MACMILLAN MODERN DRAMATISTS

Macmillan Modern Dramatists
Series Editors: Bruce and Adele King

Published titles

Further titles in preparation

MACMILLAN MODERN DRAMATISTS

OSCAR WILDE

Katharine Worth

Professor of Drama and Theatre Studies in
the University of London at Royal Holloway
College

MACMILLAN

First published 1983 by
MACMILLAN EDUCATION LTD
Houndmills, Basingstoke, Hampshire RG21 2XS
and London
Companies and representatives
throughout the world

ISBN 0–333–30422–5 (hardcover)
ISBN 0–333–30423–3 (paperback)

Printed in Hong Kong

Reprinted 1987, 1992

Contents

List of Plates

The author and publishers are grateful to the copyright holders listed above for permission to reproduce illustrations. Every effort has been made by the publishers to trace all copyright holders. In cases where they may have failed they will be pleased to make the necessary arrangements.

Editors' Preface

The *Macmillan Modern Dramatists* is an international series of introductions to major and significant nineteenth and twentieth-century dramatists, movements and new forms of drama in Europe, Great Britain, America and new nations such as Nigeria and Trinidad. Besides new studies of great and influential dramatists of the past, the series includes volumes on contemporary authors, recent trends in the theatre and on many dramatists, such as writers of farce, who have created theatre 'classics' while being neglected by literary criticism. The volumes in the series devoted to individual dramatists include a biography, a survey of the plays, and detailed analysis of the most significant plays, along with discussion, where relevant, of the political, social, historical and theatrical context. The authors of the volumes, who are involved with theatre as playwrights, directors, actors, teachers and critics, are concerned with the plays as theatre and discuss such matters as performance, character interpretation and staging, along with themes and contexts.

BRUCE KING
ADELE KING

1
A Modern Perspective on Wilde as Man of Theatre

Wilde's wit and comic genius have always been acknowledged but often grudgingly or with an undercurrent of disparagement. The early critics hardly knew how to take him. 'They laugh angrily at his epigrams', said Shaw, reviewing the first performance of *An Ideal Husband*, 'like a child who is coaxed into being amused in the very act of setting up a yell of rage and agony'. They did not grasp the subtlety of this wit. 'As far as I can ascertain' Shaw mocked, 'I am the only person in London who cannot sit down and write an Oscar Wilde play at will.'[1] A few years later *The Importance of Being Earnest* seemed to Max Beerbohm to have already become a classic; yet although greatly admiring it and indeed taking to task the actors in a revival of 1902 for reducing it to ordinary farce, he still did not get its value right; it was the 'horse-play' of a distinguished mind. Disparaging attitudes have been modified over the years but have not disappeared. W. H.

Auden praised *The Importance of Being Earnest* as the 'only pure verbal opera in English' but failed to grasp the theatrical force of the other plays, seeing only the split between the wit and the melodrama, not the provocative counter-pointing of one with the other. The theatre itself has in a way disparaged Wilde by seldom venturing on bold new approaches in production and by keeping to the 'safe' plays. *Salomé* (minus Strauss) and *A Woman of No Importance* have been almost totally neglected by professional performers.

As a corollary, perhaps, the plays have received surprisingly little critical attention. In 1969, Richard Ellmann was able to represent most of the crucial commentary touching on them in a quite slim volume. Much of the past criticism has been disguised biography or has treated the plays less as theatrical pieces than as elements in a total *oeuvre*, but now there are signs of change. An excellent modern edition of the plays, *The New Mermaids*, is appearing along with critical studies (including an account of the plays by Alan Bird) which focus on the works rather than the over-repeated details of the life.

Of course the life has to be taken into account; it was in itself a sensational drama. Wilde was born in Dublin, 16 October 1854, son of Sir William Wilde, a distinguished surgeon, and Lady Wilde, who wrote for the Irish nationalist cause under the pseudonym 'Speranza'. After graduating from Trinity College, Dublin (he acquired a lifelong love of the classics from the Provost, J. P. Mahaffy), Wilde moved on to Oxford, where, he said, life began. Loaded with academic honours, he then swiftly established a London reputation as wit, aesthete, and brilliant conversationalist and was courted by high society even before he began to publish. In 1881 he made a celebrated lecture tour of America, subsidised by D'Oyly Carte who saw the tour as a sly advertisement for *Patience*, the latest opera of Gilbert and Sullivan, which mocked aesthetes in the person of the affected Bunthorne. Wilde turned the mockery into a personal triumph; he made contacts which resulted in his first play, *Vera*, being produced in New York in 1882. He visited Paris in 1883, meeting the symbolist writers and worshipping at the feet of Sarah Bernhardt, who would have played his Salomé in London in 1892 if the play had not been banned by the Lord Chamberlain under an archaic law prohibiting the representation on stage of biblical personages.

In 1884 Wilde married Constance Lloyd; they settled in Tite Street and had two sons. He earned his living by journalism until in 1891 he published the volume of essays, *Intentions*, and other works, including *The Picture of Dorian Gray*, a novel which caused a sensation with its sinister vision of a young man's double life. Wilde's own double life (he had for some time been a practising homosexual) came dangerously into the open when in 1891 he met Lord Alfred Douglas and formed a passionate attachment to him. Between that year and 1895 he captured the fashionable London theatre with plays of modern life, beginning with *Lady Windermere's Fan*. But he was also risking his social reputation by the reckless relationship with Douglas and other affairs in the London underworld of male homosexuality ('feasting with panthers' was Wilde's phrase for these encounters). Finally, in 1895, the mounting hostility of the Marquess of Queensberry, father of Lord Alfred Douglas, erupted in the notorious card he left at Wilde's club inscribed 'For Oscar Wilde posing as a somdomite [*sic*]'. It resulted in Wilde's rashly suing Queensberry for criminal libel, losing the case, and, as homosexual relations between men were

3

illegal, finding himself on trial. In 1895 he was given the savage sentence of two years imprisonment with hard labour. While in prison he wrote a long, emotional letter to Douglas, later published as *De Profundis*. Released in 1897, he left England for France where he lived, unable any longer to function as a playwright, until his death in Paris on 30 November 1900.

In life Wilde lost the battle with 'earnestness' which in the theatre it was his mission to explode with the bombs of paradox and epigram. 'Mission' is not too strong a word, for Wilde saw the meaning of life in art and the artist as the one who was privileged to see more, able to express more, and therefore, in Beckettian phrase, under an 'obligation to express'. His view of life and art is surprisingly similar to Beckett's and to that of the other Irishmen who have changed the face of modern theatre: the artist's task was to stimulate a more intense experience by disturbing the 'monotony of type, slavery of custom, tyranny of habit, and the reduction of man to the level of a machine'.[2] Like Yeats, Wilde defined truth as a state of dynamic tension between opposites: 'A Truth in Art is that whose contradictory is also true.' He saw personality in terms of opposites, mask and anti-mask: imagery of acting and of play was to him, as to Yeats and later to Beckett, a way of expressing a profound psychological and metaphysical concept of man's nature. And like Synge, he placed enormous emphasis on the uniqueness of the individual vision: 'Still I believe that at the beginning God made a world for each separate man, and in that world which is within us one should seek to live.'[3] The artist's aim must be to convey his vision, which meant realising himself to the full, for 'the beauty of a work of art comes from the fact that the author is what he is.'

It would be no exaggeration to describe this philosophy

– life as perpetual self-creation – by the modern term 'existentialist'. There is a kind of Beckettian austerity in Wilde's unyielding insistence on the view: '. . . a thing is according to the mode in which we look at it.' Even Shaw and Yeats, both somewhat Nietzschean in their sense of the world as a product of man's energetic imagination, were disturbed by his radical vision of an all-deciding but also totally fluid self whose true mode of expression was the mask. It was a vision which found natural expression in the theatre. Wilde was the 'only thorough playwright', said Shaw, because 'He plays with everything: with wit, with philosophy, with drama, with actors and audience, with the whole theatre.' This, too, has a modern sound; 'modern' was the epithet Wilde claimed for himself, and it has not lost its appropriateness, despite the nineteenth-century flavour which is also part of his drama.

He played with the idea of the audience in near-Pirandellian style, as in the celebrated speech he made from the stage of the St James's Theatre after the first performance of *Lady Windermere's Fan* when he congratulated the audience on playing their part so well: 'Ladies and gentlemen. I have enjoyed this evening immensely. The actors have given us a charming rendering of a delightful play, and your appreciation has been most intelligent. I congratulate you on the great success of your performance, which persuades me that you think almost as highly of the play as I do myself.' This amusingly outrageous performance – made offensive to some by his casual smoking of a cigarette throughout – expressed rather more than Wilde's love of fun or his highly developed sense of publicity. He was interested at a deep level of the imagination in the piquant illustration of the image-making process provided by the actor/audience relationship. At the St James's Theatre it was especially curious. The elaborate formality of the costumes worn on George Alexander's stage reflected the clothes of the audience with a precision which made for a rather uncanny mirror image effect. Who was imitating whom? Gentlemen were said to study Alexander's immaculate dandy's outfits – of which Jack Worthing's mourning garb is the supreme example – before ordering their own clothes: presumably they thought theirs the real thing and the actors' make-believe, but Wilde knew that it was not so simple. 'Life imitates Art far more than Art imitates Life,' he announced in an article of 1889, 'The Decay of Lying'.[4] Evidence was available on the stage and off, in the couturiers' salons, the advertisement agencies, the drawing rooms, the women's magazines. When he was offered and accepted the editorship of *The Lady's World* in 1887 (his first editorial act was to change the title to *The Woman's World*), the need for money was no doubt a material factor, but the appointment was not quite so incongruous as it sounds. For Wilde did have a serious interest in women's gift for defining themselves through looks, clothes, style in general. They were doing unconsciously what the artist did with a sense of obligation, striving to create true images: 'Truth in art is the unity of a thing with itself; the outward rendered expressive of the inward; the soul made incarnate; the body instinct with spirit.'[5]

The theatre, in which all the arts of expression were gathered together, offered Wilde a peculiarly rich opportunity to express his vision of life as self-expression. Yet it was also peculiarly challenging for him. As he said, the drama was 'the most objective form known to art'. His claim, that he had made it 'as personal a mode of expression as the lyric or the sonnet', would have been endorsed by most contemporary critics, from Shaw and Archer down to the gossip columnist of the *Pall Mall*

Gazette who was struck in his own way by the 'Oscarising' of the audience at the first night of *Lady Windermere's Fan*: 'I do not remember ever being at so personal a first night. The influence of the society cynic seemed all over the house.'[6] The clash of moods and styles in his plays is sometimes extremely violent: *A Woman of No Importance* tests his skill as a synthesiser severely. But the contradictions and the drive towards synthesis are a vital feature of his art. All the plays except *The Importance of Being Earnest* (which is an exception to everything) have a strong emotional thrust towards a sacrificial climax in which love triumphs over baser passions like the desire for revenge (even *Salomé* can be seen in that light). This is not so unusual in nineteenth-century melodrama. What is unusual is Wilde's insistence on exposing this drama of feeling to the play of wit: a difficult harmonising of two modes of perception is attempted.

Wilde was a European playwright. Uniquely among the writers for the nineteenth-century English theatre he understood and responded to the symbolist movement that was exciting Paris in the 1880s and early 1890s. He loved things French and came strongly under the influence of Maeterlinck's strikingly original ideas on the application of symbolist ideas to the theatre: all the physical as well as the intellectual elements of a play were to be harmonised into a new kind of dramatic unity. *Salomé*, which owes a great deal to Maeterlinck's first play, *La Princess Maleine*, is the only completely successful symbolist drama to come out of the English theatre and it has haunted the European imagination ever since.

Wilde's aestheticism, which aroused so much notice, gossip (and, in the philistine pages of *Punch*, ridicule) was a thoroughly practical policy for the theatre. It rests upon the obvious but often unrecognised fact that audiences' responses are determined not just by what is said or done but by atmosphere, gesture, colour arrangements, and by the music and rhythm as well as the thematic content of speech. Wilde set about designing a method for making more subtle use of the physical elements of theatre. He was helped by the ideas on the dramatic potentiality of clothes, décor and music that were in the air during the 1880s. He was intimate with E. W. Godwin, father of Gordon Craig, whose 'archaeological' approach to setting and costuming inspired a whole school of theatrical exploration, and, as John Stokes shows in his valuable study, *Resistible Theatres*, provided special inspiration for Wilde. Another scholar of the subject, Ian Fletcher, suggests indeed that Wilde's speculations on costume and décor in 'The Truth of Masks' amounted to 'little more than a tesselation of Godwin's ideas'.[7] Wilde, however, as Fletcher observes, was able to take these ideas beyond the disconnected antiquarianisms or 'scholarly recreations' of Godwin and create from them a strikingly new kind of dramatic unity. Not just *Salomé* but all the plays show the marks of his 'total theatre' approach: colour arrangements and setting play a subtle part in his dramatic design; an interesting symbolism of place emerges, even in the seemingly realistic and mundane environment of the society plays. Wilde also garnered hints and ideas from Hubert von Herkomer's experiments in music theatre[8]: here Wagner was the mighty European influence. Wilde was very active in the 1880s writing and lecturing on these matters, reviewing performances of the aesthetic school, such as Lady Archibald Campbell's *As You Like It* and Godwin's *Helena in Troas*, on which he commented that there was far too much realism: when Oenone flung herself from the battlements with a 'harsh realistic shriek', said Wilde reprovingly, it was in the vein of Sardou: what the play should be aiming at was the style of Wagner's operas.[9]

Critics and directors in the past have allowed the brilliance of Wilde's dialogue to divert their attention from his scenic subtlety: so too from the subtlety of his psychological probings. In the 'plays of modern life' (especially *A Woman of No Importance*, but in them all to some extent) Wilde developed a technique of orchestrating conversation which has much in common with Chekhov's. He handles the seemingly desultory chatter of groups of people – in a ballroom, on a lawn – with delicate skill, counterpointing one style with another, hinting at sub-text through ironic contrasts, telling silences, cryptic smiles as well as through the fluent ripostes, epigrams and jokes which Wilde, as well as Freud, knew were often pointers to underlying truths about character. To Charles Ricketts he described English conversation in a quite Pinteresque way as 'rich in evasion and lit by brilliant flashes of silence'.[10] He knew too that English actors 'act best between the lines'. They lacked the French actors' ability to sustain long speeches but were 'capable of producing a wonderful dramatic effect by aid of a monosyllable and two cigarettes' ('Perhaps, after all, that is acting').[11] In the technique he evolved, this 'between the lines' style was all-important.

In comparison with Shaw (whose lectures on Socialism he attended on at least one occasion) Wilde may not seem the most politically minded of playwrights. His political essay, 'The Soul of Man under Socialism', seems to declare itself frivolous in its opening sentence: 'The chief advantage that would result from the establishment of Socialism is, undoubtedly, the fact that Socialism would relieve us from that sordid necessity of living for others which, in the present condition of things, presses so hardly upon almost everybody.' Yet the argument is in fact orthodox: altruism and charity are politically inexpedient, getting in the way of the only real solution to social ills which would be, said Wilde, 'to try and reconstruct society on such a basis that poverty will be impossible'. Years before Shaw in *Major Barbara* launched his broadside at the debilitating effects of Salvation Army charity, Wilde was announcing that 'the people who do most harm are the people who try to do most good' and 'charity creates a multitude of sins'. The aphorisms scattered through 'The Soul of Man under Socialism' could be the raw material (perhaps they were) for The Revolutionist's Handbook which Tanner flourishes in *Man and Superman*.

Wilde's revolutionary impulse was bound up with republican feeling. He remained always the son of Speranza, the patriotic literary mother whom (as Lord Alfred Douglas observed), he never ceased to revere and love. He wrote to James Knowles, the editor of *Nineteenth Century*, in 1881, enclosing a copy of his mother's pamphlet on 'the reflux wave of *practical* republicanism which the return of the Irish emigrants has brought on Ireland'. Reminding Knowles that his mother was 'Speranza' of the *Nation* newspaper, he commended her pamphlet as an interesting political prophecy, 'part of the thought of the nineteenth century', and implied support for her in his ardent comment: 'I don't think age has dimmed the fire and enthusiasm of that pen which set the Young Irelanders in a blaze'. (*L.* 80) During the period when he was writing his play about nihilism, the pages of the *Illustrated London News* were filled with pictures and commentary on the Russian Nihilists and also on the Irish troubles. 'Meath Country Gentleman Taking his Daily Constitutional' was the caption for a picture of a gentleman in his own grounds surrounded by armed guards. It is unlikely that Wilde failed to make connections between the two. His first play was about a revolutionary movement and his later plays of fashionable life can all be seen as thoroughly undermining the Victorian hierarchy.

No one can fail to notice the extraordinary preponderance of titles in Wilde's cast lists: it goes beyond anything customary in the drama of the period. Almost everybody in his plays is at least a lord or lady: his gilded beings – Hunstanton, Goring, Berwick, Darlington, Windermere – not only represent, they seem to own England. We know that Wilde tended to name his characters from places where he happened to be staying while inventing them, but the territorial grandeur accumulated by his plethora of lordships goes beyond accident. He rightly saw that in the salons and terraces where he set his seemingly frivolous plays the power of England was concentrated: and England in 1880 when he wrote his first play was the most powerful nation in the world.

In this society Wilde was an outsider. The very gifts he used to charm the class which for a time accepted and fêted him made him an object of suspicion: as Irishman, aesthete, homosexual, and above all, perhaps, as wit and artist, he was an alien among them. The prison sentence which sent him to Reading Gaol was a doom such as he had intuitively felt approaching almost from the start of his career. His expectation of suffering was, so he said in *De Profundis*, 'foreshadowed and prefigured' in his writings: 'It is one of the refrains whose recurring *motifs* make *Salomé* so like a piece of music and bind it together as a ballad.'

No doubt the sense of his own separateness, as well as his strong social compassion, is reflected in the important part played by outcasts and outsiders in his drama. There

11

is a richly varied repertoire of 'outcast' parts, from the tragic outlaws of *Vera* to the triumphant foundling of *The Importance of Being Earnest*. The motif is insistent even in the more light-hearted parts of the comedy where colonial visitors appear. An American or, still worse, an Australian will always be an outsider: riches give them admittance to society but they will be kept at the distance which the Duchess of Berwick smilingly maintains between herself and the rich Australian she is hunting for her daughter. 'Agatha has found it on the map'; so much for Australia.

True to his doctrine of opposites, Wilde was both charmed and repelled by the high life he took for material. He was repelled above all by its rigidity. A great driving force in Wilde's thinking is his antipathy to everything fixed and narrow. In 'The Soul of Man Under Socialism' he represents change as the law of life: 'The only thing that one really knows about human nature is that it changes.' The failure of some of his characters to recognise this is a root cause of their narrow, self-righteous morality. In *De Profundis* Christ is brought in as a supporter: he was the supreme individualist, the person who realised better than anyone that 'life was changeful, fluid, active, and that to allow it to be stereotyped into any form was death'. The society in the plays certainly worships stereotypes. It is only not dull and mechanical because of Wilde's witty view of it (How deadly Lady Bracknell would be in real life).

There was also a positively agreeable side to this life, which Wilde obviously enjoyed and aimed to convey. Perhaps his emphasis on the refinement, wit and elegance of their society was over-flattering to the audience at the St James's Theatre (not notable for their artistic sensibility) but it expressed a deeply held conviction of Wilde's that only when there was leisure could fineness of mind and feeling develop to the full. He saw the need for more leisure, not less, but for more people, the working class as well as the rich. His feeling about the need for individuals to realise their full potentiality was intensely religious in quality. Throughout his writings he never ceased to argue that the 'real men', the poets, philosophers, men of science and culture, were those 'who have realised themselves and in whom all humanity gains a partial realisation'. The world was formed by imagination: that was the 'world of light' and the artist should use his special gifts to enlarge that world for others – though never in the form of crude propaganda for one social system or another. The drive towards a higher state of consciousness was the purpose of life.

There was inevitably a complex relation between Wilde's humanitarianism and his artist's need for self-realisation. The humanitarianism was intensely personal: kindness was a notable trait in his character as innumerable friends testified. Even in his own dreadful situation in Reading Gaol he could feel pity and anger on behalf of prisoners more helpless and afflicted than himself and on his release he did not forget them: his open letters to *The Daily Chronicle* condemning the barbarous treatment of the child prisoners are among the most moving and effective of his polemical writings.

But self-realisation was the overwhelming obligation for the artist. And for Wilde, a sense of joy was the evidence that the process was taking its true course. Like Wordsworth, he believed that joy was the great organising principle of creation. In 'The Soul of Man under Socialism' he argues passionately that it is time for people to throw off their 'wonderful fascination' with the medieval Christian idea that pain is the mode through which man may realise himself. 'Pleasure is Nature's test,' he asserts, 'her sign of approval. When man is happy, he is in harmony with himself and his environment.'

Could these two powerful drives – towards self-sacrificing altruism and joyous self-fulfilment – be harmonised or must they be in conflict? Wilde had a visionary sense that they could be reconciled. Many pages of *De Profundis* are devoted to praise of Christ as the supreme romantic artist who exalted love and joy and yet 'regarded sin and suffering as being in themselves beautiful holy things and modes of perfection'.

A dangerous idea, says Wilde, like all great ideas: '. . . that it is the true creed I don't doubt myself.' Though it had to wait until *De Profundis* for its full elaboration, the double vision was always there. Much of the interest in Wilde's drama springs from the sensitivity and realism of his exploration into the different kinds of love and need involved in trying to be oneself and at the same time think of others.

In the treatment of women by the patriarchal society of his day Wilde found an ideal subject, both for his ideas on self-fulfilment and for his revolutionary social sentiments. Women are shown as victims in various ways, most obviously as 'women with a past' who have become social outcasts but also as the 'good women' who in effect policed society on behalf of the male Establishment. Wilde was interested in the paradox posed by these good women: they were the 'rulers of society', but the rules they enforced were against their own truest interests as free individuals. They became hypocrites in their handling of the 'double standard' in sexual matters: though they suffered from this unwritten law, they also used it to protect their position as wives and mothers. Wilde draws a great deal of comedy as well as near-tragic interest from this double effect: grossly henpecked husbands and bullying matriarchs are among

14

his funniest creations; he displays an insight of today's Women's Lib. movement in showing men too as victims of the hypocritical tyranny that made women an inferior race. Wilde recognised that this was one of the places in history to which a serious playwright must attend; it was a tender, painful and yet promising point of growth. 'Artists are the future,' he said. A change for the better in the position of women was a movement into the future in which he as an artist was fully implicated. It was a natural theme too in that it brought its own well-established theatrical form along with it. The nineteenth-century French theatre had been preoccupied with the 'woman question', from Scribe through Dumas fils to Sardou, and had worked out an elaborate and popular formula for dealing with it, the so-called 'well-made' play (this was really the old melodrama in a more refined, semi-naturalistic, middle-class form, minus the music which had played a vital part in more primitive melodramas like the English *Maria Marten* or *Lost in London*). The frailty of women or (as Henry James ironically put it, writing in 1895 on Dumas fils) 'the fathomless depravity of the female sex' was the ruling theme. James was an *aficionado* of the *boulevard* drama – when it was performed in Paris, with proper sophistication. He drew up an interesting list of the topics handled by Dumas fils, a creator of the convention. Among them were: 'the unworthy brides who must be denounced, the prenuptial children who must be adopted, the natural sons who must be avenged, the wavering ladies who must be saved, the credulous fiancés who must be enlightened, the profligate wives who must be shot . . .'.[12] Several of Wilde's theatrical situations can be spotted in this revealing inventory. Indeed the well-made *boulevard* play, in mangled translation or adaptation, was the standard fare of the London theatre in the late 1870s and

1880s when Wilde was acquiring experience as a theatre-goer. Perhaps the London theatre of the day was not quite as bad as Matthew Arnold thought it ('probably the most contemptible in Europe') but Henry James, a more informed viewer of the theatre scene in Paris and London, agreed with Arnold that it suffered from a terrible paucity of original playwrights. In transferring to the 'chill and neutral region' of London, where audiences were more *naif*, genteel and prudish than the French, plays like *Dora*, *Frou-Frou*, *Le Demi-Monde* lost both the stylistic assurance and the moral consistency of the *boulevard* convention. Situations and ideas were ruthlessly bowdlerised in a desperate attempt to extirpate 'impropriety' without losing theatrical interest.

Wilde's letters of around 1880 allude with casual familiarity to the hybrid drama so despised by James. He was happy to see the distinguished Polish actress, Helena Modjeska, in *Adrienne Lecouvreur* as well as in Schiller's *Marie Stuart* and it is clear that he kept in mind, when he came to write his own plays, many favourite situations from the French plays seen on the London stage: Sardou's *Diplomacy* (English version of *Dora*), *Odette* (Modjeska played the 'errant but repentant' wife in London in 1882), *Le Demi-Monde* of Dumas fils and his *La Dame aux Camélias* (Modjeska again, in 1880) and *Frou-Frou* by Meilhac and Halévy. It was natural for him to use the well-made convention: indeed any aspiring playwright of the 1880s was almost obliged to. James did so himself when he made his onslaught on the English theatre with *The American* and *Guy Domville*. He failed humiliatingly, perhaps because he took it so much for granted that success depended upon the playwright's willingness to use the *boulevard* form in a way which was acceptable to 'crude' English taste.

The French *boulevard* drama may have been more sophisticated than the English but its moral attitudes must strike an observer of today as thoroughly unpleasant. Even Henry James, a great admirer of Dumas fils, was uneasy about his *Le Demi-Monde*. Well he might be. The play has a classic *boulevard* situation. A 'woman with a past', a clever and superior woman, James observes, is trying to climb back into good society out of 'the irregular and equivocal circle' to which her 'faults', that is, the freedom of her sexual life, have consigned her. The only way back is through marriage to an honourable man who knows nothing of her past (if he did, he would not marry her: no questions about this in the play). Another man who has been her lover and is also the intimate friend of her suitor takes it upon himself to prevent the marriage. The ex-lover is totally unscrupulous in the means he uses to expose his unfortunate former mistress: he resorts to 'a thumping lie' (James's words) which robs her of hope and pushes her farther on the downward path. Yet he is not criticised but praised as '*le plus honnête homme que je connaisse*'. James had to admit that an English audience would not have warmed to this hypocritical and sadistic behaviour: 'The ideal of our own audience would be expressed in some such words as, "I say, that's not fair game. Can't you let the poor woman alone?" '

He was right. English audiences had their own hypocrisies, but the hard, complacent morality of the French male-dominated *bourgeoisie* was rather too ruthless for them: as James commented, they had more fundamental tenderness. Wilde therefore had more scope than his French counterparts for sympathetic treatment of 'erring' women. But he was far in advance even of the more soft-hearted among his English audiences. He continually raises provoking questions about the dogma on which the revengeful, patriarchal morality of both London and Paris was based. Should men not suffer equally with women if they have behaved badly? Still more searchingly, what is it to behave badly? Why should a society marriage arranged with an eye to money be thought morally superior to an illicit love affair? Most subversively of all, why should women not enjoy the same freedoms as men? These are the questions Wilde explores within the framework of a convention which did anything but encourage them.

In 1889 Ibsen exploded in the London theatre when *A Doll's House*, with Janet Achurch as Nora, was performed at the Novelty Theatre. Two years later, in March 1891, Elizabeth Robins, an actress much admired by Wilde, sent him tickets for the first night of her *Hedda Gabler*. He was observed by 'Michael Field' (pseudonym of Katherine Bradley and Edith Cooper) sitting in a box, watching impassively but intently. He would surely be intent. Ibsen was expressing a modern view of life such as he was aiming at himself. In April he went a second time: 'I must see your great performance again. It is a real masterpiece of art.' (*L*,291) Later he wrote to the Earl of Lytton: 'I felt pity and terror, as though the play had been Greek.' (*L*,293)

The affinity between Wilde and Ibsen was in a perverse kind of way observed also by Clement Scott, the ultra-conservative critic of *The Daily Telegraph* who notoriously described *Ghosts* in terms of loathsome sores and open drains. *Lady Windermere's Fan* could hardly provoke comparisons with open drains, but it did enrage Scott by its treatment of 'virtue'. In his review of the production, he imagined Wilde setting out to prove that the instinct of maternity, 'that holiest and purest instinct with women' could be deadened by showing 'a mother who leaves her daughter for ever, unkissed, and goes downstairs to accept the hand of a *roué*.[13] Such behaviour in Wilde's characters, Scott implied, was all of a piece with his own insolent behaviour in his speech from the stage smoking his abominable cigarette in the presence of ladies – all signs of the same moral infamy that pervaded the irreverent plays of Ibsen. As Shaw pointed out in *The Quintessence of Ibsenism*, Scott was not just an isolated fanatic in his view of what constituted virtue, especially in females. This view was widely shared: indeed it was the official view. When *Ghosts* was banned, the Censor rang the alarm against plays which inflamed public opinion by showing such things as 'dissatisfied married women in a chronic state of rebellion against not only the condition which nature has imposed on their sex, but against all the duties and objectives of mothers and wives . . .'.

In 1893, when William Archer reviewed a revival of *Diplomacy*, the English version of Sardou's *Dora*, he commented that it was not what fancy had painted it fifteen years before: 'I don't think a dramatist of today would venture to make Dora quite so humbly and enthusiastically grateful for Julian's magnanimity in offering to marry her . . . .'[14] Ibsen was one of the reasons for that change of view. And Wilde was another. The reviewer of *Lady Windermere's Fan* in the *Athenaeum* got it right when he said: 'Mr Wilde shows himself a revolutionary and an iconoclast.' It was a coincidence but what an appropriate one that the two iconoclasts had plays running at the Haymarket Theatre in the same week when the run of *A Woman of No Importance* (19 April–16 August 1893) was interrupted for three nights, for a performance of *An Enemy of the People*.

Shaw was the third in the mighty triumvirate. He proclaimed that the 1889 production of *A Doll's House* 'gave Victorian domestic morality its death-blow'. But it was Wilde (and later Shaw himself) who drove the death-blow home. Wilde was very conscious that it was two Irishmen who were waging war against English orthodoxy. 'England is the land of intellectual fog,' he wrote to Shaw in 1893 (*L*,332), 'but you have done much to clear the air: we are both Celtic, and I like to think that we are friends.' With the letter went a copy of his newly-printed *Salomé* and in return he received a copy of Shaw's *Widowers' Houses* which he acknowledged with a graceful compliment, calling it 'Op. 2 of the great Celtic School'.

Shaw's 'unpleasant' plays were produced by J. T. Grein in the new type of private theatre that began to spring up in the 1890s to meet the needs of the post-Ibsen generation. What these theatres could not supply was, as Shaw said, 'the most expert and delicate sort of acting – high comedy acting'.[15] For this a playwright had to turn to established theatres like the St James's and the Haymarket. This was what Wilde did: his campaign was to be waged at the centre of the citadel though it was a campaign of an Ibsenite kind. *A Woman of No Importance* and *An Ideal Husband* are each described significantly as 'a New and Original Play of Modern Life'. 'Modern' was Wilde's key word, but his technique was to use the old forms made familiar and agreeable to the audience through 'fine acting'. Besides melodrama, farce and burlesque were the reigning forms in the nineteenth-century theatre. Wilde was very much aware of the possibilities in these forms for modern subversiveness: 'Delightful work may be produced under burlesque and farcical conditions, and in work of this kind the artist in England is allowed very great freedom.'

His feeling about comedy was part of his philosophy of opposites. 'Never be afraid that by raising a laugh you destroy tragedy,' he wrote to Marie Prescott, the American actress, who was to play Vera, 'On the contrary, you intensify it.' 'The canons of each art depend on what they appeal to,' he went on, 'The drama appeals to human nature, and must have as its ultimate basis the science of psychology and physiology. Now one of the facts of physiology is the desire of any very intensified emotion to be relieved by some emotion that is its opposite.' (*L*,142–43). This is a remarkably assured statement from someone who at that time knew little of the theatre from the inside. Comedy was to have a subtle function in his drama, as a mode of intensifying and also of relieving feeling. Music was another such mode. Wilde's dialogue is strongly musical, markedly accented, dominated by musical devices such as repetition and variation on a theme. This is most obvious in *Salomé*, with its hypnotic beating out of obsessive *leit motifs*, but it is equally true of the comedies. Mrs Erlynne appeals to Lady Windermere to go back to her child in what can only be thought of as an 'aria', punctuated by throbbing repetitions of the name, 'Lady Windermere', and the remarkable reversal of values which comes about in *A Woman of No Importance* is given a musical summing up in a single melodic variation when the phrase 'a woman of no importance' is sardonically changed in the curtain line at the close to 'a man of no importance'.

Various kinds of music theatre, including opera, were part of Wilde's inheritance. Wagner's '*Gesammtkunstwerk*' was the great model but there was a long nineteenth-century tradition of a close relationship between plays and operas. Melodrama began as music theatre: the stage directions of the earlier, more primitive melodramas called for more or less continuous music – 'villain's music', 'wild gypsy music', 'tremolo fiddles' – as an accompaniment to the acting. The actors in melodrama continually fall into operatic groupings of choruses, duets, arias: *Lost in London* has a scene in a coal mine when the miners sing in chorus as if strayed from *Il Trovatore*. The 'well-made' society melodrama dropped the music but kept the highly accented style which had gone with it. These plays were often converted to operas; the prolific Scribe supplied Verdi with libretti for *Les Vêpres Siciliennes* and *Un Ballo in Maschera* (which has some interesting affinities with Wilde's *Vera*); Sardou's *Tosca*, a melodrama written for Sarah Bernhardt, became a libretto for Puccini's opera and *La Dame aux Camélias* of Dumas fils gained a second reputation as *La Traviata*.

The spectacular theatre too, with its *tableaux* and atmospheric scenic effects, was part of Wilde's inheritance. On all this he drew, to create for a 'modern' theatre a mode of expression 'as personal as the lyric or the sonnet'.

2
A Revolutionary Start: 'Vera or The Nihilists'

First performed 20 August 1883, Union Square Theatre, New York.
Published 1880 (privately printed), 1882 acting edition.

Those who see Wilde as a lightweight, if dazzlingly accomplished, playwright, more interested in the witty adornment of a subject than the subject itself, must find his first play, *Vera*, a considerable puzzle. What could have led the irresponsible dandy of their imagining to choose for his first venture into the theatre a theme not from the fashionable life in which he was already at home in 1880, nor yet from the romantic/historical material which was the usual choice for poets and men of letters turning to theatre at the time, but from contemporary history and a very grim piece of it: the attempts of the Russian Nihilists to assassinate the Czar. In the year before *Vera* was completed, Wilde seemed to be moving in a more

23

predictable direction: in 1879 he was proposing to Macmillan that he should translate one of Euripides' plays, possibly *Hercules* or *Phoenissae*. (*L*,59) But by September 1880 he was sending hopefully to actresses whom he admired copies of his 'play on modern Russia' which had just been privately printed at his own expense. To the American actress, Clara Morris, whom he hoped to interest in the role of Vera, he added that he had not been able to get permission for performance in London 'on account of its avowedly republican sentiments'. He was slightly exaggerating the difficulty, for the play was accepted by Mrs Bernard Beere for production at the Adelphi Theatre and should have opened on 17 December 1881 with 'Bernie', as Wilde called her, in the title role. Nevertheless his apprehension that it would not do in England was justified, for three weeks before the opening night the following notice appeared in *The World* (at that time edited by Wilde's brother, William): 'Considering the present state of political feeling in England, Mr Oscar Wilde has decided on postponing for a time the production of his drama, *Vera*.'[1]

The reason for the cancellation is not as clear as this notice might suggest. Wilde later told the American press, at the time when the play was about to open in New York, that he had not been able to find a suitable cast in London: perhaps unsatisfactory rehearsals were the real reason for the cancellation. But certainly the performance in London in 1881 of a play about the assassination of a Czar would have been rather risky. For in March of that year, the event which Wilde had imagined the previous year came about: the Czar Alexander II was murdered. The assassination received massive coverage in English journals. Portraits of the Czar and his family and of the Nihilists responsible for the murder (all were hanged) dominated the April and May issues of the *Illustrated London News*. The Czar's wife was sister-in-law of the Prince of Wales and Wilde might have felt obliged to avoid upsetting the Prince, as the production of a play so soon after the murder which could almost seem to have been inspired by it, might have done. For there are many interesting connections with historical reality in the play. Alexander II was a reforming Czar, who effected the emancipation of the serfs: Wilde's Czarevitch, too, is a reformer who is attacked by the Nihilists when he succeeds his father, whom they have assassinated.

Wilde thus showed at the start of his playwriting career his sensitivity to the high voltage points in the history of his time. Many of his sympathies and interests met in his treatment of the nihilist theme. The terrorist aspect of the movement was abhorrent to him: he shows his heroine turning away from it. But he was deeply in sympathy with the humanitarian, reforming spirit of such aristocratic Nihilists as Prince Peter Kropotkin, whom he had met ('one of the most perfect lives I have come across'), and who may have introduced him to an influential novel (available in French) by an imprisoned Nihilist. The Nihilists were congenial as an oppressed intellectual minority but above all, Nihilism would have appealed through its emphasis on freedom and the individual's right to express his individuality. Sexual freedom figured largely in the Nihilist manifesto and women's emancipation was a main plank in their programme. The Nihilist novel by Nicholas Chernyevsky, *What is to be done?*, which came out in instalments while its author was a political prisoner, presented a hero so sympathetic to women that he masochistically allows his wife complete sexual freedom while himself observing marital fidelity: this was meant as a gesture of expiation for the long subjection of women by men. Few even among his fellow Nihilists would have gone as far as this. But nevertheless Nihilism offered women, especially educated women, a chance to pursue a career, educate themselves further, travel, live their own lives.[2]

With his deep sympathy for women and interest in what the Nihilists called the 'woman problem', Wilde would clearly be drawn to the heroic, revolutionary girls whose pictures appeared in London journals about the time of the assassination. Vera Figner, a 'super-revolutionary', was also strikingly good-looking: she was arrested in 1883, having eluded capture for two years after the assassination of the Czar. In calling his heroine Vera and his Czarevitch Alexis, Wilde was keeping very close to the names of the personages in the real-life drama.

He was also close to Chernyevsky, whose heroine, another Vera, is converted to Nihilism by a young medical student. Wilde's Vera too is converted by a student, her own brother, and finds her closest affinity among the Nihilists in the young man who passes himself off as a medical student (though he is in fact the Czarevitch).

It is tantalising to think of Wilde's *Vera* so nearly missing its London production, for it does seem that conditions in London would have been more favourable to it than in New York where it was eventually produced in 1883, with Marie Prescott as Vera. It was not a success, closing after a week to notices which contained some praise but were on the whole dismissive, even rudely so. The *New York Tribune* summed it up as 'a foolish, highly peppered story of love, intrigue and politics',[3] prompting a somewhat ambivalent defence by George S. Sala, who remarked that London audiences would have felt closer to the material: they liked 'a highly peppered piece', especially with 'Russian accessories' and were passionately fond of fervid utterances about Freedom and the People'.[4]

The London production, he suggested, would also have had more visual splendour.

'Russian accessories' were prominent in the English theatre in Wilde's time. Russian themes lent themselves to 'strong' treatment; the knoutings and tortures of *Michael Strogoff*, performed in London in 1881, were, said one reviewer, 'a supper of horrors'. Opera had helped to make Russian history well known. Glinka's *Ivan Susanin* ('A Life for the Czar') appeared in 1836, and Mussorgsky's *Boris Godunov* was first performed at St Petersburg in 1874, just a few years before Wilde wrote *Vera*.

The *boulevard* playwrights were also attracted to Russian themes. Sardou's play, *Fédora*, (1882) offers an instructive comparison with *Vera*: its speciousness throws the seriousness of Wilde's approach into sharp relief. *Fédora* opens in St Petersburg. A young aristocrat, about to be married to a beautiful, tigerish princess (a part tailor-made for Sarah Bernhardt) is brought back to his apartment, wounded by an unknown assailant. The Nihilists are instantly suspected: special police appear; the spying apparatus of the Czarist state is brought into action; a 'safe' apartment is discovered, set up in well-known Nihilist style, and a suspect emerges, one Loris Ipanoff. The victim dies, and the act ends with a passionate vow of revenge from Fédora.

There is some obvious reference to real life in this opening scene: much of the detail – the Nihilist apartment, the police surveillance – seems to promise melodrama, no doubt, but melodrama with political and social as well as romantic interest. However, the promise is not realised. The scene changes to Paris and the action settles into the standard Parisian form of an intrigue drama centred on sexual passion and jealousy. Fédora tracks down Ipanoff and with the aid of the Russian secret police prepares to trap him; if she is satisfied of his guilt he will be smuggled back to Russia, presumably to be hanged. But there is a complication; she has fallen in love with him and desperately hopes to find him innocent. In the *scène à faire* she draws out the truth from Ipanoff who admits to being the killer, then baffles her by saying he is innocent. He means that he was justified because it was not a political assassination but a *crime passionel*. Fédora's betrothed had seduced Ipanoff's wife, so in killing him, Ipanoff was doing no more than avenge his wounded honour. And Fédora at once agrees that he was right: all she regrets is that he left the revenge incomplete by not killing his wife as well.

It was a London revival of *Fédora* in 1895 that provoked Shaw into his celebrated attack on 'Sardoodledom'. He was appalled by the way in which the suspected Nihilist regains Fédora's sympathy 'by proving to her that he is no Nihilist at all, but a common assassin who has deliberately murdered a man out of jealousy'. We may not feel quite so convinced as Shaw that the man who 'kills for the sake of an idea, believing that he is striking in the cause of the general weal' is more respectable than 'the dehumanized creature who stabs or shoots to slake a passion which he has in common with a stag'. But it is certainly demoralising when all the large issues drop away and we are left with a supremely trivial question: will Ipanoff remain all night alone with Fédora (to save himself) and if so . . . ? It is hard to care – about this or about the ending when Fédora takes poison in a grand 'operatic' flourish; *Tosca* without Puccini shows as bare bones indeed. Shaw began his review jokingly: 'Up to this day week I had preserved my innocence as a playgoer sufficiently never to have seen *Fedora*.' But in contemplating Sardou's handling of the Nihilist theme he worked himself up into a socialist rage, demanding, 'Why need plays be so brutally, callously, barbarously immoral as this?'⁵

Wilde had shown – many years before Shaw asked the question – that they need not be. In his letter of 1883 to Marie Prescott about the forthcoming American production of *Vera*, he explained that he had tried to express in the play 'that Titan cry of the peoples for liberty, which in the Europe of our day is threatening thrones, and making governments unstable from Spain to Russia, and from north to southern seas'. Perhaps to reassure the actress that there was a part for her, he stressed that the play was not about abstract ideas but that Nihilist Russia was 'merely the fiery and fervent background in front of which the persons of my dream live and love'. (*L*,148–9) 'Love' in Wilde's play, however, was to be a less tawdry emotion than in Sardou's. In an interview for *The World* in New York, just before the opening of *Vera*, he explained: 'Heretofore the passion portrayed in the drama has been altogether personal, like the love of a man for a woman, or a woman for a man. I have tried to show the passion for liberty. For this purpose I have chosen the most extreme expression of liberty, the Nihilism of Russia, which is akin to the anarchism of old France. All art takes an aristocratic view of life, for civilization belongs to the higher classes. I want to show how far the aspirations of an uncultivated people can be made a subject for art.'⁶

When his Vera, as a young inexperienced girl, is pressed by the peasant who wants to marry her to say whether she will ever be able to return his love, she replies, very much in the vein of Shaw's Major Barbara, 'I don't know: there is so much else to do in the world but love.' 'Nothing else is worth doing,' he replies. An ironic reversal of these points of view is brought about by the action of the play. 'The prevailing idea is a conflict between liberty and love,' Wilde said, in the interview already quoted. 'Which passion triumphs?' asked the journalist. 'That's my fifth act,' Wilde engagingly replied. It is a joke with meaning, for though he finds a theatrical resolution in his last act, the real interest in the play, as no doubt he felt himself, is in its demonstration that the conflict is unresolvable in the simple, all-or-nothing terms the Nihilists are prone to use.

Wilde was considerably excited by the step he was taking to contemporary matter and manner. 'I have gone to Greek and Gothic life for subjects for most of my poems,' he told the interviewer of *The World*, 'but my drama is from modern life. The incidents are purely imaginary, with modern Russia as realistic background.' He was anxious for the stage treatment of the first Nihilist scene to be in a modern style: the conspirators' meeting place should be bare, not an 'operatic' garret. The original 'title' for the first act was 'Tombs of the Kings in Moscow' but he changed it for the more forceful and realistic '99 Tchernavaya, Moscow' (which brings it several steps nearer to an unquestionably modern treatment of a similar theme, Conrad's *Under Western Eyes*). In all his schemes for the play's theatrical effect Wilde aimed to include a measure of realism and keep close to contemporary events: as he told the interviewer of *The World*, even the crown used in one act was 'a reproduction of the crown used at the recent coronation of Alexander III'.

The play was intended to start with the Nihilists' gathering in Moscow, but in order to obtain copyright in America (when he made his lecture tour in 1882), Wilde added a prologue, stretching the action back in time to show the origin of Vera's Nihilist passion. The scene is set in a country inn with a door opening onto a snowy landscape, a tableau highly reminiscent of the snow-enclosed landscape of *The Bells*, the melodrama which Henry Irving had been regularly reviving in London since 1871. No doubt that such melodramas were active in Wilde's imaginative processes. Dion Boucicault, Irish king of melodrama, was a friend and mentor: in the opening dialogue of *Vera*, between the peasants, the world of *The Shaughraun* is not too far off. A harrowing situation develops when a party of political prisoners in chains, on their way to Siberia, are halted at the inn for refreshment and Vera recognises one of them as her student brother Dmitri. Wilde manages skilfully here to dramatise distinctive features of the historical Russian Nihilist movement: the leading part played by students and emancipated young women; the apathy of the 'dark' peasants; the rigidity of an authoritarian régime. Nihilism is seen in a favourable light in this episode, from the viewpoint of the victims for whom no alternative is visible. Even the old father discovers a sense of injustice when he too recognises his son as the prisoners are marched off. He throws back the money the Colonel had contemptuously given and no longer exults in the fact that his inn stands on the new road to Siberia. But his indignation is purely selfish. It is left to Vera to express the revolutionary impulse in terms of a wider movement for freedom. She begs her brother to let her take his place and in a powerful melodramatic close reads from the scrap of paper he smuggles to her, giving the Nihilists' Moscow address, the chilling words of their oath: 'To strangle whatever nature is in me; neither to love nor to be loved; neither to pity nor to be pitied; neither to marry nor to be given in marriage, till the end is come.' The curtain comes down on her vow of fidelity to her brother: 'You shall be revenged!'

The play proper begins at the Nihilist meeting, 99 Tchernavaya, Moscow. Wilde's opening scene is strikingly composed to bring out a mood of tension, doubt and equivocation. In a large garret, lit by oil lamps hanging from the ceiling, a number of masked men are gathered: one, in a scarlet mask, writing; another, in yellow, guarding the door. Significantly they are described as 'silent and apart from one another'. The meeting is waiting for Vera, now a much-feared Nihilist leader. It is one of Wilde's witty strokes of invention to make the reason for her unusual delay her attendance at a masked ball in the Czar's palace. We are told that she wants to 'see the Czar and his cursed brood face to face for once'. Masks, it is clear, are to play an important part in the imaginative scheme of the play, going beyond the 'operatic' cloak and dagger procedures, to suggest the inability of the conspirators to 'see' each other aright: their individual identity is enigmatic, deceptive. So too it seems is their political identity. For Vera's former suitor, Michael, Nihilism means destruction: 'The curing of Russia is surgeon's business, and must be done by the knife.' 'Whatever *is* must be destroyed. Whatever *is* is wrong.' Alexis, the supposed medical student, has quite another aim: civilised and humane, he yearns for reform and a revolution 'not bred in crime, nurtured in murder'.

The imagery of ambiguous masking is given a spectacular and ironical turn when Vera makes her appearance. The peasant-terrorist throws off her cloak to reveal a glittering ball dress; her elegant mask links her with the aristocratic régime she loathes. The 'false' image is to prove a true one, for she and Alexis (soon to be revealed as the Czarevitch) are much closer to each other than either is to the other Nihilists. When Wilde said to the American journalist that civilisation was only possible for the higher classes, he obviously did not mean by 'higher' simply high-born; the Czar is anything but civilised.

Higher natures were what he had in mind; such are Alexis and Vera who are instinctively drawn to each other despite the immense social gap between them.

The action develops in a series of striking contrasts, from the garret (where Alexis saves the Nihilists from arrest by passing them off as 'actors') to the Czar's council chamber, a room sumptuously hung with yellow tapestry (Wilde hoped for a spectacular effect here). Windows at the back lead to a balcony where the Czar rashly ventures and is shot; a balcony figures similarly in the last act. This is a first instance of the technique Wilde later perfected for endowing rooms and other physical spaces with symbolic value.

In this elegant setting Wilde introduces Prince Paul Maraloffski, his wittiest invention in the play, and obviously a prototype of the later dandies: some of his best lines, like 'Experience, the name men give to their mistakes', turn up again in the society comedies. He provides a tart, sceptical perspective on the idealists, seeing the Prince as an ingenuous young man who 'preaches socialism, and draws a salary that would support a province'. Each moral attitude has its own verbal or 'musical' style and they are provocatively counterpointed, the Czar and his son indulging in throbbing rhetoric which draws from Prince Paul the tart comment: 'Heroics are out of place in a palace.' The heroics have it, however. The Czar's paranoia reaches its head: swearing war on the people 'to their annihilation', he rashly ventures onto the balcony, a shot is heard and a voice crying 'God save the people'. The Czar dies, screaming at his son that he is the murderer.

In the third act the Prince, sent into exile by Alexis, the new Czar, seeks out the Nihilists, for now his mission in life, like theirs, is revenge. In strokes of telling irony Wilde shows how easy it is for this extreme right-wing politician to find common ground with the extreme left-wing. He does not even need to simulate any commitment to democracy but, on the contrary is mockingly frank about his aristocratic prejudices: 'I hate the common mob, who smell of garlic, smoke bad tobacco, get up early, and dine off one dish.' When faced in a typically melodramatic ritual with the choice of a dagger (meaning his own death) or the paper inscribed with the Nihilist oath, he amusedly indicates that of course there is no real choice: 'I would sooner annihilate than be annihilated'.

Throughout this sequence, in which Prince Paul comes near to reducing the Nihilist rituals to farce, Vera stands by, separated from her 'brothers' by her inability to accept, as they do, this unlikely new member. No one seems any longer to speak her language. Wilde points up this idea through an audacious contrast between her rhetorical organ notes and the Prince's light mocking tones:

VERA: Welcome! What welcome should we give you but the dagger or the noose?

PRINCE PAUL: I had no idea really that the Nihilists were so exclusive. Let me assure you that if I had not always had an entrée to the very best society, and the very worst conspiracies, I could never have been Prime Minister in Russia.

Wilde takes an obvious risk here – Vera's rhetoric could easily be pushed over the edge of the absurd by the Prince's cool reasoning. Yet it does not quite happen, perhaps because her style is after all more in tune with the violence of the play's events.

The rhythms of melodrama become steadily more

pronounced as the Nihilists drive towards the assassination of the now detested Alexis and the lot falls on Vera. Agonised, she takes up the dagger which she is to throw down to her fellow conspirators with Alexis' blood on it (otherwise they will storm the palace to kill the Czar themselves). Cloak and dagger stuff, but as Lord Alfred Douglas commented (on another of Wilde's plays), melodrama does occur in real life. Readers of the *Illustrated London News* in 1881 knew that it did; they would be familiar, as we unhappily are today, with the 'melodramatic' methods adopted by contemporary terrorists, including paranoiac checks on their own members. That this melodrama, with all its *rhodomontade*, is happening in the real world, we are reminded by the cool presence of Prince Paul, who welcomes the drawing of lots as the first piece of business to enliven the meeting and reflects sardonically on the likely outcome: 'This is the ninth conspiracy I have been in in Russia. They always end in a *voyage en Sibérie* for my friends and a new decoration for myself.'

In the final act the language becomes ever more 'Shakespearean' as Wilde tries desperately to raise it to the level of the lovers' feelings. The Czar starts to behave as if he were in one or other of Shakespeare's history plays but is not quite sure which, while Vera enters his room where he sleeps as though she had strayed from *Macbeth*: 'One blow and it is over and I can wash my hands in water afterwards.' She is raising the dagger to strike when he wakes, pours out his love, tells all he has done for her sake, including freeing the political prisoners, and begs her to marry him. The anarchist recoils – Vera the Empress of Russia! – but the woman responds with delight. It is the climax Wilde has been preparing from the start, the triumph of love, but in the spirit only, for throughout the scene the murmuring of the Nihilists is heard beneath the window, grim reminder that the lovers are hopelessly trapped.

Wilde pulls out all the stops for this high moment, drawing more heavily than ever on Shakespeare. Vera rhapsodises like Juliet over her 'wedding night', while Alexis responds like a prosaic Othello with 'I could die now'. The language remains leaden; still, that does not prevent the action from rising to its heroic climax when, to save her lover, Vera kills herself and so is able after all to throw down a bloodstained dagger to the inexorable comrades. Dying, she cries, 'I have saved Russia.' The vow taken at the start of the scene has been fulfilled in a way which brings out the complete reversal of her Nihilist philosophy. 'Saving Russia' now means valuing the individual above the group, reform above violent revolution, love above revenge and hate. The conflict between love and liberty has been resolved in a sacrificial act. It is melodrama still, but one that Wilde certainly meant to be taken seriously.

It would be hard to claim that *Vera* was a quite satisfactory play: even in terms of the convention in which Wilde was working, the language and action are inflated, sometimes beyond the bounds of plausibility. This is not a case of a neglected masterpiece. Yet the play has much interest. The wit is of the sort seldom found in melodrama, least of all the Sardouesque kind. Wilde's intellectual grasp of political concepts gives his sensational human drama some depth and subtlety: one is certainly grateful for the provocative changes of perspective Prince Paul's sharp scepticism brings into the play.

Vera is also Wilde's first attempt at a technique of total theatre. He was deeply involved with theories of decoration and colour at the time of writing: the setting and costumes in the play are clearly meant to be more than decorative. The bold yellows and reds which dominate the first Nihilist scene are picked up again in the striking yellow of the Czar's council chamber ('The yellow council chamber is sure to be a most artistic scene,' Wilde wrote to Marie Prescott) and in the brilliant vermilion of Vera's dress. Hidden affinities between the seemingly alien and opposite camps are thus hinted at, as masks are used to suggest ambiguous and concealed motives among the conspirators. Arresting tableaux were a feature of melodrama, but Wilde's scene of Moscow under snow ('How white and cold my city looks under this pale moon and yet what hot and fiery hearts beat in this icy Russia'), like the tentative patterning of movements from room to room, is the beginning of the 'place' symbolism which he was to perfect in *Salomé* and the plays of modern London life.

The dialogue too is orchestrated in a way which contributes to the total theatre technique. The operatic chorus of Nihilists chant in unison; characters step forward from time to time to deliver arias and there are some complex musical arrangements in contrasting speech styles, as for instance the 'trio', with the Czar hysterical, Prince Paul light and mocking, the Czarevitch icy and self-controlled. At such moments the play is close to the melodramas which so easily converted to operas, and indeed to the operas. *Vera* has much in common with Verdi's *Un Ballo in Maschera* (1859) which was adapted from Scribe's melodrama on Gustavus III of Sweden. It, too, has an assassination, tangled personal and political passions and many confusions of identity, wittily (and eventually tragically) expressed in a masked ball. And it had the same trouble with censorship: the assassination of Napoleon III made the performance in Italy dangerously inflammatory. (The problem was solved by an absurd change of setting to Boston.)

Wilde frequented opera and could well have had *Un Ballo in Maschera* in mind. He was also one of the *avant garde* who in the 1870s were enthusiasts for Wagner. There are hints in *Vera* of Wagnerian influence: changes of mood and feeling are signalled by changes in rhythm and speech forms. (When the rhetoric thickens, modern forms are replaced by archaic ones, as 'hath' for 'has': Vera is particularly drawn to this usage.) Biblical phraseology and Shakespearean quotation are consistently used to change to a deeper key. The linguistic method of *Salomé* is anticipated here.

If we think of it as a play for today, *Vera* presents all kinds of awkward problems: its melodrama might well defeat modern actors, though if performers with the right skills could be found, the play might well emerge as an interesting stage piece in its own right. It is certainly important as a revelation of Wilde's early ability to take up the thematic and theatrical material of his time and give it more subtle form, close to opera but also anticipating the later plays in witty and modern treatment of character and ideas.

3
'The Duchess of Padua'

First performed 21 January 1891, New York.
Published 1908.

This is the one completed play of Wilde's which can scarcely be imagined in a modern performance. He himself, when looking for a work to dedicate to Adela Schuster, told Robert Ross that *The Duchess of Padua* would not do: 'It is unworthy of her and unworthy of me.' (*L*,757,fn.) It is his most heavily derivative play (Shakespearean echo is taken to the point of the ludicrous) and it is written in blank verse, decidedly not his medium. Yet, although crippled as an acting piece by such defects, it retains interest as a revelation of Wilde's thinking on themes that were important to him and on the staging methods which he hoped would realise them.

The American actress, Mary Anderson, was interested in the play, and it seemed as if she would perform it in New York (in October 1883). She changed her mind, telling Wilde that she feared the play 'would no more please the public of today than would *Venice Preserved* or *Lucretia Borgia*'. (*L*,142,fn.) It was an accurate prophecy. When *The Duchess of Padua* was produced in New York in 1891 by Lawrence Barrett, under the title, *Guido Ferranti*, it had a very short run (21 January to 14 February) and the reviews were lukewarm at best. It was taken on tour by Minna Gale but although she saw the Duchess as a starring role, she annoyed Wilde by performing his work less often than the others in her repertoire, of which *Romeo and Juliet* was one, by curious coincidence; that play is prominently in the background of both *Vera* and *The Duchess of Padua*.

What, then, are the points of interest in *The Duchess of Padua*? In the first place there is Wilde's choice of subject. The play is set in the Renaissance but it was clearly influenced by Shelley's *The Cenci*, a revolutionary modern treatment of Renaissance material that had a strong appeal for the avant garde of the 1880s (banned by the Lord Chamberlain, it was given a private performance by the Shelley Society in 1886). Wilde told Mary Anderson that he expected his play to excite audiences by its modern approach: 'They will not expect to find in an Italian tragedy modern life: but *the essence of art is to produce the modern idea under an antique form*.'[1] Shelley was a key figure in Wilde's pantheon and *The Cenci* expressed most of the sentiments the two writers had in common, including passionate devotion to freedom.

The similarities between the situations of the two plays are striking enough to make Wilde's seem at times a copy of Shelley's. His central character, a young, beautiful woman, is the sexual property of a tyrant old enough to be her father; a euphemistic, late Victorian version, one might say, of Shelley's horrific situation: the rape of Beatrice Cenci by her actual father. Wilde's heroine too is called

Beatrice (after starting life as Bianca); she too is finally
provoked into murdering her tormentor. Here, however,
the resemblance ends, for Wilde's Duchess escapes the
grasp of the law which sadistically destroys Beatrice Cenci.
In a curious reversal of Shelley's situation she steps into
the position of power vacated by the man she has
murdered and clears herself by denouncing her young lover
as the murderer. It is the lover, Guido Ferranti, who is
brought to trial (in a set-piece scene which seems to
emulate the gloomy grandeur of the Cenci trial) and is
sentenced to death. Finally, the Duchess makes an effort to
save him but it is too late; all she can do to atone is to take
the poison which has been laid out for him; he finds
another way to kill himself and they die together in a
tableau which like much else in the play points irresistibly
to *Romeo and Juliet* as another potent influence.

Initially the dramatic focus is on Guido Ferranti: he
arrives in Padua, an unworldly, impulsive young man,
drawn to the city by the sinister Moranzone, who is
described by Wilde (in the letter to Mary Anderson, an
important document for the reading of his mind) as 'the
incarnate image of vengeance: the bird of evil omen; the
black spectre of the past moving like Destiny through the
scene'. Moranzone reveals to Guido the secret of his birth:
he is really the son of the great Duke Lorenzo who was
treacherously handed over to an ignominious death – 'in
common fetters bound' – by the man who now reigns as
Duke of Padua. Moranzone appoints Guido as avenger,
shows him his dead father's dagger and tells him he will
receive it as the signal to murder the Duke. Guido
undertakes the charge: Wilde comments that he is 'full of
noble ideas but "Fortune's fool" '. 'Fortune's fool' is
what Romeo calls himself after he has killed Tybalt and is
forced to fly from Verona and from his love. Guido too,

41

Wilde hints, is to be seen as 'star-crossed', divided from his love by the 'black spectre of the past' which is totally given up to hatred. As in *Vera*, the passion of hatred is brought into conflict with the passion of love – and again love triumphs, though it leads nowhere but to death.

The first act ends with the appearance of the Duchess, a vision of beauty under a canopy of silver tissue. Guido and she look at each other, the dagger drops from his hand and it is clear that they have fallen in love at first sight. He asks who she is and the reply forms the curtain line: 'The Duchess of Padua'. Wilde expected this line, coming as the culmination of the scene, to create a novel and striking effect: it was, he said, the keynote of the play.

In the second act the conflict of love and hate begins. Guido, now in the Duke's service and biding his time for his revenge, is deeply in love with the Duchess. She is starved of love. That is Wilde's justification of the murderous acts she commits later in the play, so it is important for him to establish her early misery convincingly. His method of doing so makes a strong link with *Vera*. The Duchess suffers personally and also on behalf of the people of Padua who are treated with ruthless contempt by the tyrannical and cynical Duke. When she impetuously distributes her purse among the Duke's wretched petitioners, the act draws a cold storm from her husband: she spreads rebellion, has made the common people love her: 'I will not have you loved.' The Duchess has been placed in a position which almost requires her to take action against so inhuman a husband if she does not wish to emulate that character of Browning's who seems to have been in Wilde's mind, the divinely forgiving Pompilia.

Wilde's Duchess has not that saintly capacity. Like most of his heroines, she is a modern woman in spirit, resentful of men's domination, vigorous in pursuit of her own fulfilment. When Guido appears, offering his love, he soon draws from her an admission that she too fell in love the first moment they met, and though her virtue is not in question, it looks as though she would seize her chance of sexual joys, when the dark shadow of Moranzone falls across them. Guido receives the signal (the dagger, symbolically wrapped in vermilion silk), reluctantly separates himself from the Duchess, telling her only that there is now a 'barrier' between them, and nerves himself to commit the murder, already seeing the 'bloody hands' that will never afterwards be free to make love to her.

The distraught Duchess turns on Moranzone when he reappears – all in black, like a revenger in a Jacobean tragedy – and threatens him with torments if he persists in exerting his malign influence:

> Or I will tear your body limb from limb,
> And to the common gibbet nail your head
> Until the carrion crows have stripped it bare.

This is an unexpected side of the patient Griselda whom her husband abuses at will. It is a pity the language of the scene is generally so florid, for it masks the interest of the psychological exploration Wilde is attempting. He shows that the two lovers, though they talk of union and understanding, are in fact separated by total ignorance of each other's nature. She has no idea Guido is hag-ridden by the thoughts of revenge, nor he that his idealised 'white Duchess' is capable of such ferocity.

A gigantic gulf opens up between them in Act 3. Guido decides not to commit the murder but instead to lay the dagger by the sleeping man, with a letter telling 'who held him in his power/And slew him not'. This will be a form of 'noble' vengeance. At the head of the staircase, his hand on the crimson *portière*, he is confronted by a figure in white, his 'white and spotless angel', who tells him that the 'barrier' has been removed in a 'steaming mist of blood'. A rather horrific colour effect, this, which Wilde was to return to in *Salomé*.

Guido is totally horrified; he turns a deaf ear to her plea that she did it for love of him, softening only when it is too late; she has sent her soldiers to arrest him as the murderer, a disconcerting *volte face* indeed. In Act 4 the Duchess becomes a real White Devil (Webster was obviously in Wilde's mind, as well as Shelley). She tries to stop Guido from speaking in his own defence and expresses regret that his head was not struck off the moment he was seized. 'Art thou that Beatrice, Duchess of Padua?' he asks with understandable incredulity. 'I am what thou hast made me,' she replies ('the keynote of Act 4' says Wilde). Yet he still loves her. When he is allowed the opportunity to speak out, he heaps coals of fire on her head by supporting her story: he alone is the murderer.

What would have happened if he had told her sooner that he loved her despite the horror of her deed? This, to Wilde, was the crux of the play, as he told Mary Anderson, again drawing a comparison with *Romeo and Juliet*: ' "If Guido had only spoken sooner": "if Juliet had only sooner wakened": "too late now" are in art and life the most tragical words.' Strangely, he assumes that the responsibility for the tragedy rests on Guido. He reacted, says Wilde, with a 'sternness, which is right, but unsympathetic'. But is it? Are we really prepared to gloss over not only the killing but, still more difficult, the Duchess' treachery to her lover? Can we possibly agree with Wilde that, when she expresses her despair at Guido's rejection of her by denouncing him to the guard, 'every woman in the audience will say to herself "I would have done likewise" "? It is one of the rare moments where Wilde seems to falter in psychological understanding. He told Mary Anderson that it was necessary to take a scientific approach to characterisation. Audiences were well-meaning but very stupid, always needing to have their vague emotions crystallised for them. He was writing to her at such length to show 'how scientifically I have thought out this matter in all details'. Yet it hardly seems very reasonable to expect sympathy for the Duchess at the moment when she falsely accuses her lover of the murder she has committed herself. The explanation lies in Wilde's idea of the Duchess as 'an image of pity and mercy'. In Act 2, when she 'comes with the poor about her', he was sure that she would stir the sympathy of the gallery and pit: 'In London, where the misery is terrible among the poor, and where the sympathy for them is growing every day, such speeches as the one about the children dying in the lanes, or the people sleeping under the arches of the bridges, cannot fail to bring down the house.' (*L*,137)

Wilde would have liked that speech printed on the advertisements for the play, substituting 'in this city here' for 'in Padua', to make the social point in both London and New York, like Dion Boucicault's *The Streets of London*, which changed its name wherever it played. As so often, Wilde is working within the melodrama tradition at its most popular and socially sensitive. He sees the Duchess as another Vera; it is Wilde the social revolutionary and admirer of Shelley who demands sympathy for her as a crusader on behalf of the under-privileged and also as a woman who is herself a victim of male tyranny.

The death of the lovers, the Duchess drinking the poison meant for Guido, he stabbing himself with her dagger (having first reproached her for leaving no poison), is glaringly derivative. But as always with Wilde, there is a tough, realistic element too. He conveys the panic of a young woman who suddenly, realising what she is losing, shrieks, in physical agony, that she will not die, and offers to give Padua away to any doctor who will gain her one more hour of life. It is a painful and grotesquely harsh scene, as Wilde realised, for he explained to Mary Anderson that it was too violent to be sustained to the end: 'She must not die with wandering mind, and diseased vision, and physical pain stifling her utterance. That would be too material, too physical an ending for a work of spiritual art.' Instead she dies talking of forgiveness, questioning Guido about her chances of salvation. The once stern moralist has gone to the other extreme and will forgive her anything: 'They do not sin at all/Who sin for love.' So she is after all the one who arrives at a truer perspective:

> No, I have sinned, and yet
> Perchance my sin will be forgiven me.
> I have loved much.

The final tableau seems to offer a silent benediction. Whether it worked on stage one can only guess, but Wilde's intention is clear. The Duchess dead in a chair, her cloak falling like a shroud around her, Guido lying outstretched across her knees, form a secular *Pietà* (her face is a 'marble image of peace'). Sexual love has been given a supreme endorsement, brought closer to the maternal relationship which for Wilde was the type of selfless love.

The mood throughout the play is intensely religious. Christ is continually invoked, as in the Duchess' dying allusion to the biblical saying, 'Her sins, which are many, are forgiven; for she loved much.' Perhaps uneasily aware that the result was over-emotional, Wilde stressed to Mary Anderson the need for comedy to provide a firm intellectual underpinning. He gives the Duke some insolent and, as he says, 'bitter' comedy and there are occasional flashes of wit elsewhere, with a bit of laboured, sub-Shakespearean jesting from the lower orders. However, Wilde's wit is in shackles here, no doubt weighed down by Renaissance themes and quasi-Shakespearean verse. More happily, the play shows his grasp of the physical aspects of theatrical art even at a time when he had no experience in the theatre. He had a very clear idea of how he wanted the stage to look. The opening scene – a market place in Renaissance Padua with coloured awnings, Romanesque cathedral in black and white marble, fountain sporting a green bronze triton – could be an antiquarian reconstruction such as audiences of the 1880s enjoyed in the Shakespearean productions of Tree or Irving, and in the aesthetic experiments of Godwin. So too with the other scenes, all of which have features which suggest historical actuality: stamped grey leather on the court-room walls, gold and silver plate, and so on.

But it is clear that Wilde's design is meant to have more than archaeological interest. As he said himself in 'The Truth of Masks',[2] antiquarianism only becomes alive when it is made part of the dramatic process. So when he indicates that the dungeon scene should include a group of gambling soldiers who might produce 'a sort of Salvator Rosa effect', he is trying to take the scene away from the 'depressing gloom' of out-and-out naturalism and create a mood appropriate to the spiritual intensity of the lovers' world. So with the colour scheme: it is in tune with the reds and golds of Italian Renaissance decoration, but is also highly symbolic. Red is the dominant. Despite his sympathy for the Duchess, Wilde knew that the horror of her actions had to be fully registered in the aesthetic texture: 'Now, murder is murder, a dreadful thing . . . it becomes the bloody background of the play and we must not dim its scarlet.' The vermilion silk containing the dagger, the crimson *portière*, the scarlet robes of the judges suggest the 'thin red stream of blood' that flows between the lovers and the 'red fire of passion' that caused the blood to flow. Red, white and black form changing patterns. Moranzone, in black, casts the brooding shadow of revenge over the action. The Duchess wears white and walks beneath a canopy of silver (Guido calls her his 'white Duchess') but she is attended by pages in scarlet. There is a corridor of red marble in the ducal palace, the Cardinal is in scarlet, so too the Lord Justice, glimpsed in the dungeon scene in a carefully composed frame; two openings into the dungeon allow first a head and shoulders and then a three-quarter length view of the grim procession which brings the Headsman to his victim.

Wilde has the strongly developed visual sense frequently found in the writers of nineteenth-century melodrama: it often has a filmic quality, as in the framing scene just mentioned and in the murder scene of Act 3 when the curtain rise reveals a shadowy, enigmatic picture which slowly comes to life as the light changes, revealing the masked figure draped in black sitting at the foot of the great staircase. Light is used to give *chiaroscuro* effects: by the flickering torch and the flashes of lightning which along with thunder accompany the scene, we receive glimpses of violently contrasted views; the city of Padua seen through a great window, peaceful in the moonlight, and the staircase that leads up to the crimson *portière* masking the entrance to the victim's bedroom. One of the most startling and momentous visual effects in the play was to be the sudden appearance of the Duchess, all in white, against the crimson of the *portière*, after she has murdered the Duke. Wilde gave much thought to the means of creating this spectacular scene: crimson velvet, his first thought, was changed for vermilion silk which, he suggested, would catch the light better and be altogether more effective in producing the image he imagined, a 'door of crimson fire'.

Sounds too were to contribute to the pattern. The tolling bell in the last act, Wilde assured Mary Anderson, would be the 'most musical bell in the world'. The purely aesthetic appeal of glowing colours and musical sounds was obviously strong for him; but his advice on staging is not that of a self-indulgent hedonist. Rather, it reveals a clear idea of how aesthetic elements could contribute to the expression of a serious theme. The visual beauty is on one level simply realism. It would be natural for a state room in a Renaissance palace to have its walls hung, as in Act 2, with tapestries picturing the Masque of Venus. But the Venus scenes also provide a silent endorsement of the beauty Wilde claims for the passion of Guido and the Duchess.

This visible beauty, so much in contrast with the grim action, raises questions about the place of art in life. 'Love will bring music out of any life,/Is not that true?' the Duchess asks Guido in their first love scene. 'Sweet, women make it true,' he replies, and goes on to compare women's capacity for love with the power of the artist which has transfigured the Renaissance world they both inhabit:

> Women are the best artists of the world,
> For they can take the common lives of men
> Soiled with the money-getting of our age,
> And with love make them beautiful.

In this high estimate of woman as artist – an artist whose medium is life itself – Wilde answers the question which the plot forces on his characters: What gives life its value? 'Love' is the greatest good, and women have the key to it. He was to hold fast to this thread, even in the sophisticated modern comedies, even in the next and strangest of his plays, *Salomé*.

4
'Salomé'

First performed 11 February 1896, Théâtre de l'Oeuvre, Paris.
First performed in London, 10 and 13 May 1905, New Stage Club at Bijou Theatre.
Published 1892.

Salomé was the one play of Wilde's to receive the 'accolade', as Shaw considered it, of banning by the Lord Chamberlain. The play had got as far as rehearsals at the Palace Theatre, with Sarah Bernhardt already knowing what she would wear as Salomé (blue hair and her Cleopatra dresses), when the licence was refused, because – as Wilde sardonically put it – 'no actor is to be permitted to present under artistic conditions, the great and ennobling subjects taken from the Bible.'[1] There was dismay and incredulity in many quarters. William Archer, defender of Ibsen, protested that England needed Wilde (He had reacted impulsively to the ban by threatening to leave London for Paris), 'to aid in the emancipation of art from the stupid meddling of irresponsible officialdom'.[2] The French seized the opportunity to mock English philistinism, proving their own superiority in this respect by allowing the first performance of the play in Paris (in 1896, when Wilde was in prison[3]). Wilde was given a sympathetic interview by the *Pall Mall Budget* in which he stressed his detachment from the philistine race: 'I am not English; I'm Irish – which is quite another thing.' But of course the Lord Chamberlain had the backing of the Establishment – *The Times* criticised the play when it was published as 'an arrangement in blood and ferocity, morbid, bizarre, repulsive, and very offensive in its adaptation of scriptural phraseology to situations the reverse of sacred'.[4] And there was silence from the English theatre world. Wilde pointed this out to William Rothenstein: '. . . not one single actor has protested against this insult to the stage – not even Irving, who is always prating about the Art of the Actor. This shows how few actors are artists.' (*L*,317)

Paris had a certain appropriateness as venue for the première of *Salomé*. Wilde wrote the play in French, anticipating his fellow Irishman, Beckett, who also turned from English to French (and back again). And he had been excited at the thought of a French actress – 'the greatest on any stage' – playing his heroine. Yet the Frenchness of *Salomé* is only skin deep. Philippe Jullian suggests that when the play is performed in French it has to be spoken with an English accent, so as to bring out key words with the right force.[5] The English translation has no less status than the French text: Wilde let Alfred Douglas put his name to it, but the common assumption that he revised the Douglas translation to the point where it became his own is surely right.

How did Wilde come to write this strange play? Part of

the answer does lie in Paris and in Wilde's fascination with
the symbolist writers and painters who encouraged him in
his intuitive sense that the stage should be 'the meeting
place of all the arts'. Rhythm, musical language, colour,
lighting, dance, were to produce a 'concrete' imagery of
the stage in a style approved by the French and Belgian
symbolists. The Irish were especially responsive to this new
movement: Yeats, in Dublin, was also pursuing a vision of
total theatre inspired largely by symbolist Paris and the
Belgian Maeterlinck. However, *Salomé* does not stand
outside Wilde's *oeuvre*, as a thing apart. No doubt his
interest in total theatre techniques was stimulated by his
association with the French avant garde (in 1891 he was
spending a good deal of time in Paris taking advice on the
correctness of his French from Pierre Louÿs and the
symbolists) but it had manifested itself long before, in
essays like 'The Truth of Masks', in his reviews of
'aesthetic' productions such as Lady Archibald Campbell's
Coombe Park *As You Like It*, and in his own early plays.

In *Salomé* Wilde was able to realise ideas which had
been tentative or abstract in *The Duchess of Padua*: the
symbolic colour scheme, for instance, and the recurring
allusions to Christ as the symbol of love. In the new play
Christ is 'really' there, an off-stage character, forgiving
sins by the Sea of Galilee, able to forgive Salomé, so
Jokanaan tells her. The heavily rhythmic cadences and
biblical phraseology of *Salomé* also recall the style of *The
Duchess of Padua*, though blank verse has been
abandoned for prose, one happy result of the play's being
written in French.

The style of *Salomé* is also coloured by a very different
play of Wilde's which he was writing more or less at the
same time. He told Alexander in the February of 1891 that
he had not yet been able to 'get a grip' on the new work he

53

had promised ('Artistic work can't be done unless one is in the mood'). (*L*,282) Called at that time *A Good Woman*, it emerged later in the year as *Lady Windermere's Fan*. It is one of the most striking proofs of Wilde's versatility that he was able to let the witty idiom and worldliness of the modern play penetrate the sealed, intense world of *Salomé*, where it sets up interesting reverberations. Herod has a modern self-consciousness, and Herodias would be quite at home among the tart dowagers of Lady Windermere's society.

There is yet a third style at work in *Salomé*. This one is French – or rather, Belgian, for although Maurice Maeterlinck wrote in French, the atmosphere he creates is distinctively of his own country, viewed through a symbolist prism. Wilde was immediately attracted to Maeterlinck's mystical plays. The first one, *La Princesse Maleine*, was published in 1889 in Ghent (and rapturously praised by Octave Mirbeau who hailed the new playwright as the Belgian Shakespeare). Wilde was invited to write an introduction to the English translation which Heinemann published in 1892. He is quoted as saying that he would have to wait for inspiration. It never came, so far as the introduction was concerned, but it certainly came in the form of stimulus to his own creativity in *Salomé*. There is plenty of evidence for Wilde's interest in Maeterlinck. Only two modern playwrights really interested him, he once told a journalist, Victor Hugo and Maeterlinck.[6] When explaining why he chose to write *Salomé* in French, he quoted Maeterlinck as an instance of the special or 'curious' effect that came from writing in a language not quite one's own ('He, a Flamand by grace, writes in an alien language').[7] Years later, when friends were allowed to supply him with reading matter in Reading Gaol, his requests included the entire works of Maeterlinck. But we need look no further than *La Princesse Maleine* to recognise how deeply Wilde was influenced by the Belgian symbolist. In both plays a very young heroine is overwhelmed by a passion which drives her inexorably to a violent death. The mysterious relation between love, sin and suffering is a major theme in both: the mood is tragic, fatalistic. Maeterlinck's play is loaded with Shakespearean echoes, from plays which had always figured largely in Wilde's imaginative life, *Romeo and Juliet* and *Macbeth*: these reverberations are felt also, though less obviously, in *Salomé*.

Maeterlinck's frail little princess and Wilde's commanding, alluring one might seem to have nothing in common. But they have: it is natural for Wilde's treatment of his heroine and her story to reflect something of the Maeterlinckian approach. Maleine, though gentle, is obdurate: she cannot be turned from her desire. Fragile, nervous (her panic as death approaches is painfully real), yet she knows that her fate is to be joined in love with Hjalmar. And they are joined, though only in death. Wilde's heroine, also described by the young Syrian who worships her as a 'little princess', is similarly overwhelmed by the first passion she experiences: it is instantaneous and irrevocable:

Ah, Jokanaan, Jokanaan, thou wert the only man that I have loved. I saw thee, Jokanaan, and I loved thee.

The feelings would be appropriate to Maleine (or to the Juliet who so haunted Wilde's imagination). By the time the lines are spoken we have travelled far from the world of those other heroines: Salomé utters them to the terrible object she has demanded from Herod and now holds in her hand, the severed head of the beloved. But still, even in the midst of the horror, there remains the poignancy of the young girl's single-minded longing and her despair: if we do not feel this at the end of *Salomé* we have not experienced Wilde's play.

Wilde's reasons for choosing the story of Salomé have been much debated: as in the genesis of any work of art many different factors were no doubt involved: Richard Ellmann, for instance, interestingly identifies the violently contrasting sexual philosophies of Ruskin and Pater as a germinating force. More obviously there was the popularity of the Salomé topic with *fin de siècle* artists: she was obsessively painted by Gustave Moreau, Klimt and others. And there were models provided by Flaubert and Mallarmé, and Massenet's *Hérodiade*. There is also, however, a less recognised but important point of departure in *The Duchess of Padua*. We need to register this, I believe, to account for Wilde's so different attitude towards his subject from that of his French contemporaries. Where they emphasise the exotic and perverse elements in the fable – Salomé as the symbol of decadence – Wilde sees her far more sympathetically as 'the tragic daughter of passion'. To find an explanation we need only look back to the scene in *The Duchess of Padua* when the Duchess is repulsed by Guido after she has told him that she has murdered her husband. She too pleads for love from a censorious character who backs away, saying 'No, do not touch me', very much as Jokanaan shouts at Salomé 'Back! daughter of Babylon'. The Duchess too turns hysterical and vengeful in the agony of her thwarted love: she too imagines her lover's head being struck off 'with an axe' and does bring about the sentence of execution, symbolically represented in the last two acts of the play by a looming, ominous headsman.

Cruel sexual frustration in its turn begetting new cruelty

was, then, a theme Wilde had already explored; it was obviously important to him, as when he took up the story of Salomé, he turned it in the direction of *The Duchess of Padua*. The biblical Salomé has no sexual motive: she dances for the head of John the Baptist simply, it seems, at the instruction of Herodias. The subject was also a good choice for Wilde in that it provided a language for the 'strong' emotions he was driven by inner forces to express. The biblical cadences suited him. He could be musical without falling in to the blank verse trap, and 'music' was what he aimed at. He used a musical metaphor in explaining why he wrote the play in French: 'I have one instrument I know that I can command, and that is the English Language. There was another instrument to which I had listened all my life, and I wanted once to touch this new instrument to see whether I could make any beautiful thing out of it'.[8] When the play was in rehearsal in 1892, with Sarah Bernhardt as Salomé, Wilde reacted to her performance as though she were a supreme musician rather than an actress. He heard 'the most beautiful voice in the world' interpreting his music. (Although he had not written the play for her – that approach was for the artisan, not the artist – hers was the perfect voice for Salomé.)

Maeterlinck had introduced a new kind of musical speech, bringing very simple little words into a rhythmical texture which had Shakespearean overtones but a modern prose idiom. Repetition was an all-important feature of the technique. Simple, even banal, phrases in *La Princesse Maleine* acquire fatalistic intensity by being repeated in a helpless, hypnotised way. Characters seem compelled to use the same words, move in certain directions, enact rituals they hardly understand – always in a scenic context alive with enigmatic 'meanings'. Wilde evidently drew hints from this strange language, as from the complex scenic scheme in which the landscape has a voice and changes of sound or colour presage the catastrophes of the human drama.

There are remarkable likenesses in the opening scenes of *La Princesse Maleine* and *Salomé*. Maeterlinck's play begins with bystanders superstitiously connecting the stars and comet which seem to rain down on the castle with the death of princesses. The sky darkens, the moon becomes 'strangely red' and Maleine runs out from the castle, in tears at the breaking up of her betrothal by the grossly drunk and lecherous old King Hjalmar. *Salomé* opens on the great terrace of Herod's palace. The stage directions – more laconic and selective than in the earlier plays – specify a balcony; a 'gigantic staircase' (by which Herod enters and departs); an old cistern surrounded by a wall of green bronze. And: 'Moonlight'. Here too characters are looking at the sky, reading omens and thinking about a young princess. The page (in love with the Syrian captain, as he is in love with Salomé) has premonitions of death: 'Look at the moon! How strange the moon seems. She is like a woman rising from a tomb. She is like a dead woman. You would fancy she was looking for dead things.' Into this Maeterlinckian scene, comes an agitated princess, also fleeing an unseemly uproar tolerated by a sensual king whose lechery is threatening and incestuous: 'It is strange that the husband of my mother looks at me like that.'

The first impression of Salomé, then, is of a girl fiercely defensive of her virginal integrity. Looking up at the brilliant moon, she exclaims: 'The moon is cold and chaste. I am sure she is a virgin, she has a virgin's beauty. Yes, she is a virgin. She has never defiled herself.' When the voice of the prophet rings out of the cistern, prophesying some violent purification, she feels an instinctive affinity. She persuades the adoring Syrian to bring him out of the cistern and it is love at first sight, as in Wilde's favourite *Romeo and Juliet*. It is as if he were seeing what might happen to that desperate intensity of adolescent love if it were not reciprocated but repelled with ferocious distaste for the very idea of sex. In this first phase of the action (dominated by the white moon), the two virginal beings confront one another and Jokanaan repels her with neurotic intensity: 'Who is this woman who is looking at me? I will not have her look at me. Wherefore doth she look at me with her golden eyes, under her gilded eyelids?' Once he hears her name he panics: 'Back! Daughter of Babylon! Come not near the chosen of the Lord.' He has only one tone of voice, an organ note always thundering. It is a measure of his grandeur and rigidity: he is trapped in the narrow role of prophet, cannot change, cannot really listen to what other characters say. His monotone becomes a Maeterlinckian device for creating a feeling of doom: he knows at the beginning that death is coming: 'I hear in the palace the beatings of the wings of the angel of death.'

An impression of doom is created too by the ritualised wooing of Jokanaan. Like the moon, which hangs over them all so menacingly, Salomé must go through three phases: white, red and black. It is his whiteness she first adores: 'Thy body is white like the lilies of the field that the mower hath never mowed . . . . Let me touch thy body.' When Jokanaan repels her ('Back! daughter of Babylon! By woman came evil into the world') she unsays, in the manner of a curse, all that was beautiful in the idea of whiteness and substitutes all that is horrible: 'Thy body is hideous. It is like the body of a leper . . . . It is like a whitened sepulchre full of loathsome things.' So with the motif, black. First, an image of fertility: 'Thy hair is like clusters of grapes, like the clusters of black grapes that hang from the vine-trees of Edom in the land of the Edomites.' Then, the opposite: darkness of mire and dust, hair 'like a crown of thorns'. Finally, red. His mouth is a band of scarlet on an ivory tower, 'a pomegranate cut with a knife of ivory'. Red, colour of wine, fruit and blood invades the other colours and all its shades seem to be concentrated in the passion of her last appeal: 'Let me kiss thy mouth.'

He repels her for the third time, for everything must happen in threes under the spell of the triple Hecate, or Cybele, the goddess seen by one critic, C. S. Nassaar, as the presiding deity of the play.[9] It is the sense of fatality and of the wasted capacity for passion which raises Salomé's drama to the level of tragedy. When she refuses to accept her rejection, her obstinate repetition of the line 'I will kiss thy mouth, Jokanaan,' has something childish about it (the spoilt girl *will* have her way) but is invested with a rather terrifying dignity and force by the intensity of the ritual which has gone before. The young Syrian recognises that the inexorable repetition of the dread line, 'I will kiss thy mouth,' has the ring of doom in it. He makes one despairing attempt to turn her back to the Salomé of his amorous vision – 'the dove of all doves' – and when he fails, kills himself. His body falls between Salomé and Jokanaan and the page is heard mourning the death of his beloved. All Salomé can see is the object of her desire, as unattainable as the young Syrian for the page or Salomé herself for the Syrian. In this one sequence Wilde has concentrated a whole volume of unfulfilled longing.

In the second phase, of the red moon, Jokanaan descends into the cistern, still protesting as he goes that he will not look at Salomé, and there is a spectacular quick cutting to the entrance of Herod and Herodias, she scolding him for looking at Salomé too much: 'You must not look at her! You are always looking at her!' A new psychological realism and complexity comes into the play with Herod. He has been taken as a self-portrait and no doubt does express his author more fully than any other single character in the play. Aubrey Beardsley's fantastic illustrations for the published text slyly make that point: Wilde's features appear in Herod (though also in Herodias and the Woman in the Moon).[10] In the first English production of *Salomé*, the part of Herod, as played by Robert Farquharson, was found by far the most fascinating: Ross recalled that even those who disliked the play and its author (they were many in 1905) were 'hypnotised by the extraordinary power of Mr Robert Farquharson's Herod'.[11] Richard Ellmann suggests that Wilde projected through Herod his own ambivalent attitude to the extremes represented by Jokanaan and Salomé, also his ability (more wished for than complete) to maintain a safe distance from the violent beings who so attracted him.

All this is in the background of the character through whom Wilde developed persuasively for the first time his concept of masks; the idea that personality necessarily swings between opposite poles. In Herod the contradictions are extreme. He is a gregarious extrovert: the intense inwardness of the opening scene is shattered when he makes his noisy entrance with his retinue and quarrelling wife, bringing in variety, colour, tumult. Yet he is capable of self-scrutiny as no other character is. He is sensual, abandoned, florid: the moon (by which they all define themselves) is for him a drunken, naked woman, reeling through the sky in search of lovers. Yet he is deeply respectful of the ascetic and spiritual nature: he listens intently as the Jews debate the nature of God and he

defends the prophet against them, as against Herodias:
'This man comes perchance from God. He is a holy man.
The finger of God has touched him . . . . God is always with
him.' Typically he has to add 'At least it is possible. One
does not know.' Always he is pulled in different ways. He
is superstitious (it is 'a very evil omen' when he slips in the
young Syrian's blood on entering the stage) and so
histrionic that it is hard to know how seriously to take him.
Yet he has true intuitions, sensing the approach of some
malign event the moment he enters the terrace:

> HEROD: It is cold here. There is a wind blowing. Is there
> not a wind blowing?
> HERODIAS: No; there is no wind.
> HEROD: I tell you there is a wind that blows . . . And I
> hear in the air something that is like the beating of
> wings, like the beating of vast wings. . . .

He has much in common with Herodias, but whereas she is
perfectly at home in the mundane world, he is restless
there. He is the first of Wilde's characters to be self-
conscious in a thoroughly convincing and interesting way,
the only one in the play who turns on himself the 'look'
they are fated to turn on each other. It is a moment of
bitter self-consciousness that Salomé's horrific demand
forces from him: 'Your beauty has grievously troubled me,
and I have looked at you too much. But I will look at you
no more. Neither at things, nor at people should one look.
Only in mirrors should one look, for mirrors do but show
us masks.' The contrast between this complex, vacillating
character and unimaginative Herodias provides a vein of
comedy which is remarkably unexpected in such an intense
symbolic drama.

The prophet becomes a pawn in the marital conflict, a

trigger to the bickering of the dreadful pair. The 'incest' which Jokanaan sees in Old Testament terms – 'Ah! The wanton! The harlot! . . . Let the people take stones and stone her,' – is for them just an ordinary marriage with some built-in guilt and irritation, but no more than she at any rate can deal with in a perfectly mundane way. Jokanaan gives this henpecked husband a rare opportunity to score off his wife. 'He speaks never against me,' Herod says complacently, 'Never has he spoken word against me, this prophet, save that I sinned in taking to wife the wife of my brother. It may be he is right. For, of a truth, you are sterile.' The insult draws from her vituperation in the same style, ending with a taunt, 'It is you who are sterile, not I.' This is domestic realism: it lowers the tension, allows the audience to take a cooler view, appropriate to interesting, rather unpleasant characters in a satirical comedy. It is a necessary relaxation before the tremendous climax and it ensures that the characters are seen as real people, not images or symbols, as the fanatical Jokanaan and Salomé incline to see them.

At the climactic moment when Salomé consents to dance for him (in return for his promise to give her whatever she asks 'even unto the half of my kingdom'), Herod reminds himself of the danger of pursuing obsessive images. 'You must not find symbols in everything you see,' he tells himself; a moment of rather poignant irony, for the self-recognition is too late. Blood imagery dominates now, and as in the earlier plays, strong echoes from *Macbeth* are heard. 'What is it to you if she dance on blood?', sneers Herodias, when Herod agonises over the idea of Salomé's naked feet treading in the Syrian's blood: 'Thou hast waded deep enough therein.' Then the moon turns red. We may imagine every figure and object on the stage bathed in sinister red light when Salomé enters and, as the bald stage direction has it, 'dances the dance of the seven veils.'

The dance is an enigmatic event. How it would have been done by Sarah Bernhardt at the Palace Theatre, who can tell? Voluptuous in *fin de siècle* style, presumably. Graham Robertson, in charge of the costume designs, tells how she planned to use costumes from her sumptuous Cléopâtre (Robertson designed a gold dress for her, with breastplate and triple crown) and insisted on having the blue hair which Wilde intended for Herodias.[12] She meant to perform the dance herself. This astonished even Robertson, an uncritical admirer, and is certainly hard to envisage; she was nearing fifty and had never been a dancer. Of course the dance comes, as it were, with the story: many exotic images had been invented for it by artists like Moreau; Loie Fuller, idol of the symbolists, danced the role in her characteristic swirling greens and blues, using mirrors to multiply the image of the dancer. Wilde was susceptible to *fin de siècle* exoticism, especially to the symbolic jewellery which figures so prominently in Moreau's seductive paintings and Huysmans' celebrated description of Salomé's lascivious dance in *A Rebours*: 'Her breasts quivered and at the touch of her whirling necklaces of jewels, the nipples rose; diamonds, attached to the dampness of her flesh, scintillated; her bracelets, her girdles, her rings gave out sparks. . . .'

Herod's great panegyrics on his collection of precious stones (seen by Wilson Knight as part of a consistent 'jewel' symbolism) are verbal arias which it might well have pleased Wilde to see matched by an ornately jewelled dancer. He did describe his play as Byzantine (rejecting Beardsley's 'Japanese' interpretation) and Bernhardt was the 'Byzantine queen of Paris'. Probably anything she did would have pleased him.

However, he had in mind a colour scheme for the play so much more modern than Bernhardt's Cleopatra style that one wonders if he would not have preferred a more modern approach to the dance also. 'I should like everyone on the stage to be in yellow,' he told Robertson, who was deeply impressed ('I saw the possibilities at once – every costume of some shade of yellow from clearest lemon to deep orange . . .'). Robertson patronisingly assumed, deceived like so many by Wilde's light touch, that the brilliant notion was 'random'. In fact Wilde's visual ideas were more inventive and consistent intellectually than those of the designers and actor-managers he worked with. Charles Ricketts, who created a much-admired décor for the 1906 production of *Salomé* (by the Literary Theatre Society), could not remember whether it was he or Wilde who had planned 'masses' of colour for the original design, with the Jews all in yellow and Herod and Herodias in blood-red. The stage floor was to have been black to show up Salomé's white feet, moving 'like doves'; the sky 'a rich turquoise blue, cut by the perpendicular fall of gilded strips of Japanese matting, forming an aerial tent above the terraces'. Significantly, Ricketts fancied Salomé in conventional *fin de siècle* gold and silver. Wilde saw her 'green, like a curious, poisonous lizard'.[13] These designs, as Philippe Jullian rightly says, 'went beyond Art Nouveau, and heralded those of the Russian Ballet'.[14]

A dancer from the Russian Ballet could have created the right sort of dance for *Salomé*. Wilde said himself that he would have liked the character played by an actress who was also a first-class dancer, and he evidently thought hard about the dance. An account written after his death has him swinging between two seemingly opposite views of it: in one Salomé is the seductress, entirely naked except for cascades of exotic jewels; in the other a 'blazingly innocent' Salomé wears veils 'woven by angels'.[15] These are the contradictions in the character herself, of course, and a reflection of Wilde's ruling principle: 'A truth in Art is that whose contradictory is also true.'

Unlike Yeats, who had the good fortune to attract Ninette de Valois to dance for him, Wilde had no opportunity to influence stage interpretations of his dance. The early English performances, according to Max Beerbohm, were genteel (Salomé in the first production was 'a thoroughly English young lady').[16] Later performances tended to the conventionally exotic, even, as in many of the dances inspired by Strauss's music, rather tawdry; Graham Robertson noted that the Salomé dancer in the opera was usually a commonplace figure, running in and out of her palace 'half-naked, in the flimsy muslins of an Eastern dancing girl'. Strauss's music is thrilling, but it does encourage an extrovert idea of the dance as totally sensual and seductive, a misleading view, as I have suggested.

Wilde had in mind a more inward meaning, as is implied in his inscription in the edition he presented to Aubrey Beardsley: 'For Aubrey: for the only artist who, besides myself, knows what the dance of the seven veils is, and can see that invisible dance.' Imagery of veiling and unveiling is frequent in Wilde's prose writings and is usually associated with some kind of spiritual exploration. In the short story, 'The Fisherman and his Soul', for instance, a girl with a veiled face and naked feet is one of the images that lures the Fisherman back to his alienated soul. Unveiling was an appropriate image for the activity which Wilde regarded as the artist's primary duty: self-expression and self-revelation. In performing the dance of the seven veils, Salomé is then perhaps offering not just a view of the naked body but of the soul or innermost being. Even Maud Allan, a dancer of Wilde's time, who performed 'her' dance of Salomé in music halls and emphasised the spectacular elements, was highly sensitive to the visionary aspects of the story and tried to suggest these in her performance. She entitled the second part of her dance 'The Vision of Salomé' and represented the whole episode with the severed head as a kind of phantasm, rather as Moreau had shown it in his picture, 'The Apparition', where a possessed Salomé looks up to a mystical severed head, hovering like a dream above her. Wilde may not have known how the symbolic effect he wanted could be achieved in physical terms but a sufficiently imaginative dancer could surely find the means. In the present day theatre Lindsay Kemp has given a completely Wildean interpretation, effecting the transformation of a middle-aged, balding dancer into the young princess by the strength of his vision of the Salomé in himself. ('I *am*, inside, the most beautiful woman'.) When he abandoned all theatrical aids – glamorous costume, wig and so on – and performed the final sequence in his own person, he amazingly achieved that inner transformation and self-revelation with which Wilde was fundamentally concerned. It is Salomé alone in the play who offers this experience.

Throughout the play the characters have looked at each other and been baffled by unyielding surfaces which, like mirrors, have only thrown back the reflection of the self. Herod is given the chance to 'look' at Salomé as she is in her inmost being. But he cannot read what he sees. A 'charming' girl he is calling her, even as she begins – surely without charm – to tell him what she wants brought to her on a silver charger. When he hears what it is – 'the head of Jokanaan' – he is completely stupefied. The shock drives him into the play's most elaborately wrought piece of orchestration, which echoes the triple pattern of Salomé's ritualistic pleading with Jokanaan. In three sumptuous arias, he pleads with her to take in place of what she asks first, the largest emerald in the world; second, his white peacocks; third, his collection of jewels. It is in a way a vulgar display, an ostentatious peacock-flaunting and revelling in luxury: 'I have topazes, yellow as are the eyes of tigers, and topazes that are pink as the eyes of a wood-pigeon, and green topazes that are as the eyes of cats.' Yet, as in the character of the voluptuary who owns these treasures, there is a vein of poetry and mysticism in the display. Each beauty has some shadow to it, all are under the fatal power of the moon and reflect an imaginative world in which everything is created from within. Among the fabulous jewels are turquoises which give the wearer the power to 'imagine things which are not'. This is the dreaming process in which all the characters (except unimaginative Herodias) are involved. In his way Herod is revealing his own nature, full of contradictions, inspired by beauty and haunted by fear of death.

He shows a true intuition in his final offer to the dancer who has unveiled herself. 'I will give thee the veil of the sanctuary,' he shrieks, drawing cries of sacrilege from the Jews. He is out of his depth, for he has no power to make such an offer, but he knows that this is the language appropriate to Salomé's desires.

Always there is returned to his flowing periods a staccato sound, monotonous, relentless: 'Give me the head of Jokanaan.' That sound brings his sonorous music to a close. After all the words, a nightmarish silence succeeds: in silence the death ring is passed to the executioner; he goes down into the cistern and Salomé leans over, hears only silence, though 'something' falls. Then, still in

68

silence, an extraordinary tableau is revealed. Out of the cistern rises the huge black arm of the executioner holding on a silver shield the severed head of Jokanaan. There is blood on the head; we must envisage this, not for purposes of realism, but because the showing of the head is really a surrealist composition in white, red and black, the symbolic colours of the moon: we are in the depths of the mind, experiencing a Dionysiac vision.

Herod had said that the sight of the severed head would be unfit for 'the eyes of a virgin'. The subterranean implication that the head symbolises the sexual organs comes to the fore when Salomé takes the horrific object in her hands and expresses a savage lust: 'Ah! Thou wouldst not suffer me to kiss thy mouth, Jokanaan. Well! I will kiss it now. I will bite it with my teeth as one bites a ripe fruit.' Here, if ever, she comes close to seeming inhuman, a savage sex goddess. But it would be a simplification to see her only in that way. She is victim as well as destroyer: it is the relation between her frustration and her manic passion which Wilde is especially concerned to explore.

The final sequence is still in triple form. First, she releases all her pent-up rage and frustration, mocking the closed eyes and the tongue, once a 'scarlet viper that spat its venom upon me', gloating: 'Well, Jokanaan, I still live, but thou, thou art dead, and thy head belongs to me.' The savagery effects a kind of catharsis: the poison is out, and she can move into a stiller, sadder music, through the imagery of the past recreating the Jokanaan who might have loved her. White, red and black remain, but only as emblems of beauty; all the dark, perverted side has disappeared: 'Thy body was a garden full of doves and of silver lilies . . . there was nothing in the world so black as thy hair . . . . In the whole world there was nothing so red as thy mouth.' That is her elegy for him. At last, in the third phase, she confronts again her own feeling. It is raw, full of pain: 'Ah! ah! wherefore didst thou not look at me, Jokanaan? If thou hadst looked at me thou hadst loved me.' She is still the immature girl, pathetically sure that she should be able to have her own way, if only . . . . Yet there has been a maturing all the same. She has learnt to the full what passion is and she has learnt through her suffering the value of love. We cannot forget the horror that came of her agony – she is cradling the head throughout her speech – but by the end she is accepting her wounds, no longer trying to wound. It seems, against all the odds, that 'love' is the right word for the feeling she achieves after the cruel passion has spent itself and that, as she says, 'the mystery of love is greater than the mystery of death. Love only should one consider.'

None of this deep movement in the soul, and into the 'mysteries' is perceived by Herod. Salomé has become for him a monster; her crime against 'an unknown god' will bring some doom on him. In superstitious terror he abandons all attempts at 'looking' which by this stage of the play must be equated with vision and self-scrutiny. 'Put out the torches! Hide the moon! Hide the stars!' he shrieks: 'I will not look at things, I will not suffer things to look at me.' In a last spectacular piece of symbolism the lights go out on the stage, the torches are extinguished, the stars disappear and a great black cloud crosses the moon and conceals it. Blackness has completed the pattern: out of the dark sounds the voice of Salomé telling that she has achieved (with what bitter irony) her desire: 'Ah! I have kissed thy mouth, Jokanaan. I have kissed thy mouth.' A single moonbeam falls on her 'covering her with light', an equivocal direction. The effect on Herod is to increase the frenzy of fear which leads to the horrific climax: he orders the soldiers to kill her and they carry out his command in a great stylised act of brutality which is the fulfilment of the prophet's grim forecast. They 'crush beneath their shields', says Wilde, 'Salomé, daughter of Herodias, princess of Judaea.' It is nemesis; yet, as the direction 'covering her with light' suggests, also a kind of violent release from the dark, corrupt world which has disfigured Salomé's passion: the value of love is proclaimed, even in the savage departure from it. Wilde said of his life that it stood in symbolic relation to his age. In *Salomé* he achieved for the first time in his drama the fabulous quality his personal story was to acquire. And the fable asserted the primacy of love.

The symbolic force of *Salomé* was felt at once in Europe. Perhaps even the clumsy English censorship was an obscure recognition, a shrinking from the dionysiac experience. Lugné-Poe hastened to present the play in Paris, justifying Wilde's belief, proclaimed at the time of the ban, that the French were more civilised: it was some solace to him in his misery in prison that the 'tragic daughter of passion' was being given her voice on a European stage. The translation into opera followed swiftly after; in 1905 Richard Strauss recreated it in musical terms so thrilling that the opera has ever since put the play into the shade. Wilde might have considered that metamorphosis to be no more than a particularly full realisation of his 'musical' idea, for the opera does not depart from the text (except by truncating it): all the great moments are his. But wonderful as the opera is, it cannot totally satisfy those who admire the play: much has been dissolved away in Strauss's insistently erotic syncopation, for instance the humour and irony of the relationship between Herod and Herodias, and all those inner subtleties which Wilde's more varied rhythms reveal.

The play has fascinated even those who disliked or were

nervous of it. Yeats professed to despise its dialogue ('empty, sluggish and pretentious'), but could not keep his mind off the haunting image of the dancer with the severed head. He rewrote *Salomé* not once but twice, as *The King of the Great Clock Tower* (1934) and *A Full Moon in March* (1935), admitting that it was 'a fragment of the past I had to get rid of'. With curious symmetry, the dancer who played Yeats's dancing Queen, Ninette de Valois, later choreographed the dance in *Salomé* for Terence Gray at the Festival Theatre, Cambridge, and for Peter Godfrey at the Gate Theatre, when Constant Lambert provided new music and Margaret Rawlings was Salomé. Beatrix Lehmann, who was Terence Gray's Salomé, impressed one reviewer so much by her fine balance of feeling and 'stylised' movement that he asked, 'How, one wonders, could this play have ever been banned?' This in 1931 when censorship, public and private, still kept its grip.

Perhaps Wilde's play contributed to the change in consciousness which has come about in our era. It has certainly continued to inspire performances of great originality, in the newer media of film and television as well as in the theatre. Wilde would surely have been impressed by the French television production which created a remarkable realism through its bleak Israeli desert landscape and threatening cistern, without forfeiting rhythmic grandeur. So too, in a different way, he would have enjoyed the balletic version by Lindsay Kemp: the all-male company half acting, half dancing the play, speaking now in English, now in French, created some unforgettable images – the ravaged splendour of Herodias, Herod's sinister seductiveness, the transvestite Salomé, whose stripping of the veils was in the nature of things obliged to be a revelation of spirit rather than body, the 'idea' or essence of Salomé.

'Salomé'

Salomé remains Wilde's master work in the symbolic mode; a spiritual concept completely realised in a dramatic structure of intense physicality and in this way 'modern' as he claimed; the first triumphant demonstration of the symbolist doctrine of total theatre.

5
'Lady Windermere's Fan'

First performed 20 February 1892, St James's Theatre.
Published 1893.

'Time: the Present'. The opening stage direction of *Lady Windermere's Fan* proclaims that Wilde had parted company with the operatic/symbolic: he had stepped to the centre of the London stage, launching himself and George Alexander of the St James's Theatre into a phase new to both. Under its original title 'A Good Woman' the play had first been offered to Augustin Daly – Wilde envisaged Ada Rehan in the star part of Mrs Erlynne – but it was Alexander, just become manager of the St James's, who took up the opportunity (Hesketh Pearson says it was he who first persuaded Wilde to turn his hand to 'modern comedy'). A partnership began which allowed Wilde to exploit to the full his keen existential sense that all life was acting and that to be conventional was especially 'to be a comedian'.

1891, when he wrote *Lady Windermere's Fan*, was the

year of Ibsen in London. In the spring Wilde had seen
Elizabeth Robins in *Hedda Gabler* and been so impressed
that he asked her to arrange for him to see it again: she
was, he told her, an ideal exponent of the play's subtlety
and tragedy and her performance was 'a real masterpiece
of art'. Ibsen too had turned from romantic historical
drama to a modern art which he once described as
'photographing' his contemporaries. Photography is at
once the right and the wrong term for Wilde's new drama
also. It is right for the special illusion of real life which
greatly impressed the first reviewers of *Lady Windermere's
Fan*: 'That morning room, with its rich brown panels, was
a triumph. It looked so like a room, and so unlike a stage
imitation of one.'[1] There was also the startling closeness,
already observed, between the actors and the audience,
who included, as one reviewer said, 'pretty women and
exquisites . . . and a score of faultless young dandies'. The
audience was made to feel at home in the St James's
Theatre on 20 February 1892. They might have felt at
home too, at any rate for a time, with the dramatic
situation of the play. This tale of a 'woman with a past'
seeking to re-enter society and thereby almost precipitating
her daughter into a fate like her own clearly had kinship
links with the Anglicised *boulevard* drama of Paris which
was standard fare for fashionable London audiences.[2]
Wilde's treatment of the material, however, changed it
radically. *Lady Windermere's Fan* is 'A Play about a Good
Woman' structured so as to undermine the conventional
notion of 'good'. What that is we are shown in the opening
scene between Lady Windermere and Lord Darlington. He
caddishly hints that her husband has become the intimate
friend of a woman 'of – well, more than doubtful
character' and invites her to agree that in such a situation
the wife should console herself. Lady Windermere

responds with right feeling but ominous exaggeration – 'Because the husband is vile – should the wife be vile also?' – and when he asks if women 'who have committed what the world calls a fault' should never be forgiven, has no hesitation in saying they should not be, nor men neither. Life would be much simpler, she naïvely pronounces, if everybody kept to the 'hard and fast rules' which Lord Darlington rejects.

It is difficult to be sure at this point what sort of man her would-be lover is. But it is clear that Lady Windermere's intolerance has to be related to her youth (the ball to which her husband insists on inviting the 'doubtful' Mrs Erlynne is in honour of his wife's twenty-first birthday) and the excessively sheltered life she has led. The truth about her mother (who ran away with a lover at the age she now is) has been kept from her and a false image of an 'ideal' mother who died young planted in her mind. She is also encouraged to be pharisaical by society: the dowagers find it convenient to measure respectability by whether or not the strict young wife offers anyone a card, as the Duchess of Berwick makes clear in the first act when she announces that Lady Windermere's is 'one of the few houses in London where I can take Agatha'. Lord Windermere, pleading with his wife to admit Mrs Erlynne to her ball, puts it in the same way: 'She knows that you are a good woman – and that if she comes here once she will have a chance of a happier, a surer life than she has had.' This is what society has ordained as Lady Windermere's role: it is a fearfully apt nemesis when the narrow virtue encouraged by the husband recoils on him. 'How hard good women are,' he sulks when his wife adamantly refuses an invitation to Mrs Erlynne.

We can hardly blame her, for by this time, under the influence of the gossip-mongers, she has broken into her husband's desk (her virtue already crumbling) to find what seems hard financial evidence of his affair with Mrs Erlynne. He will not tell her the money he is paying out is going to his mother-in-law, not his mistress. (Contemporary reviewers sympathised with Alexander for having to play a 'good' man among so many cynical ones – a curious view of Lord Windermere's moral attitude.) Lady Windermere becomes wild with jealousy, threatens to strike Mrs Erlynne at the ball and, though she does not, the sight of the stranger so intimate with her husband, determines her to go to Lord Darlington as Wilde says, for 'protection'.

In the third act her education in moral feeling begins. By this time the audience know who Mrs Erlynne really is (Alexander persuaded Wilde to reveal the secret earlier than he had originally planned), and can appreciate the complex pain of the scene, when Mrs Erlynne follows her still unknowing daughter to Lord Darlington's rooms to save her from making a mistake like her own of twenty years before.[3] Wilde traces the movement of Lady Windermere's mind with exactness. It is clear that she has little real feeling for Lord Darlington: 'Why is he not here,' she says petulantly, when she enters his apartment to find it empty, 'to wake by passionate words some fire within me?' Though still resentful of her husband's infidelity, she resolves to return to him. It is only the arrival of Mrs Erlynne, begging her to do what she has already decided to do, that changes her mind: she will stay, not, as the *Pall Mall* critic thought, with a 'determination to dishonour her husband', but for the opposite reason; she cannot bear the hypocrisy of the arrangement Lord Windermere seems to have made with Mrs Erlynne ('My husband sent you to lure me back that I might serve as a blind to whatever relations exist between you and him') and would prefer it all out in the open, even if there were to be 'the worst scandal there has been in London for years'. Mrs Erlynne recognises that her daughter 'couldn't stand dishonour': this is one of the arguments she uses in a long impassioned speech in which she pleads with her to return to her husband and child. She succeeds. There is a touching moment when Lady Windermere appeals to her almost as if she instinctively recognised their relationship: 'Take me home, take me home.' Then the crisis; Lord Darlington's return with a bevy of friends, including Windermere and Lord Augustus Lorton (whom Mrs Erlynne has practically landed as a husband) pushes the play nearer the 'well-made' convention, though not for long. Desperate at the thought of being discovered in a bachelor's apartment late at night, the women hide themselves (Lady Windermere in Lady Teazle style behind the curtain, Mrs Erlynne in an off-stage room – presumably the bedroom).

They thus become eavesdroppers on a male conversation which, like their own, though in very different tone, turns on the obsessional theme of 'good women': 'That is the worst of women. They always want one to be good. And if we are good, when they meet us, they don't love us at all. They like to find us quite irretrievably bad, and to leave us quite unattractively good.' The witty *aperçu* is given a sentimental turn by Lord Darlington, still brooding over his rejection by Lady Windermere. The woman he loves (he looks at Windermere as he speaks) is 'good' *because* she doesn't return his love. 'She is the only good woman I have ever met in my life.' He does not get much encouragement. 'The only good woman you have ever met in your life?', says Cecil Graham, 'Well, you are a lucky fellow! Why, I have met hundreds of good women. I never seem to meet any but good women. The world is perfectly packed with good women. To know them is a middle-class education.' 'This woman has purity and innocence,' Darlington persists, 'She has everything we men have lost.' Graham laughs him down: 'My dear fellow, what on earth should we men do going about with purity and innocence? A carefully thought-out buttonhole is much more effective.'

The audience must be with the cynic. Lord Darlington's sentimental moralising is the worst sort of hypocrisy. Would he still be rhapsodising over Lady Windermere's purity if he knew she was there in his rooms? Would any of the men believe in it if she were to emerge from behind the curtain? We know the answer, for we see their reaction to Mrs Erlynne when she steps out to save Lady Windermere (who slips away unobserved) from being discovered through her carelessly dropped fan. It is a silent tableau of ostracism: 'Lord Windermere looks at her in contempt. Lord Darlington in mingled astonishment and anger. Lord Augustus turns away. The other men smile at each other.'

The fourth act, back in the Windermeres' house, shows Lady Windermere's education achieved. The immature convictions of the first act have given way to a panicky realisation of fallibility: 'How securely one thinks one lives – out of reach of temptation, sin, folly. And then suddenly – Oh! Life is terrible. It rules us, we do not rule it.' Paradoxically, it is now, when she is shattered, that we see the real strength of her character. Even if Mrs Erlynne continues to sacrifice herself and keep silent, Lady Windermere resolves that she must tell her husband the truth of what happened the night before. In three sequences dense with thought Wilde shows his understanding of his characters' psychology, while keeping an ironic focus on the imperfections of society which make them behave as they do. First there is a duologue between Lady Windermere and her husband in which she defends against his contempt the woman he once defended against her. When he says that Mrs Erlynne is 'bad – as bad as a woman can be', her response shows how far she has advanced: 'I don't think now that people can be divided into the good and the bad, as though they were two separate races or creations.' The irony is sharp, for he has come to believe Mrs Erlynne worthless at the very moment when she has shown her worth. He always was cool to her (Wilde wanted the actor who played the part to be courteous but hard in his second act scene with her). But his new harshness is unpleasant: he does know, after all, that he is speaking of his wife's mother.

In the second duologue, between Mrs Erlynne and Lord Windermere, the irony becomes more harsh and bitter. Lord Windermere spares her nothing: she is 'disgraced before everyone' and her attempt to get back into society, for which he originally felt sympathy, he now interprets as the lowest of actions: 'One day you read in the papers that she had married a rich man. You saw your hideous chance. You knew that to spare her the ignominy of learning that a woman like you was her mother, I would endure anything. You began your blackmailing.' She fights back with customary aplomb: 'Don't use ugly words, Windermere. They are vulgar. I saw my chance, it is true, and took it.' But she knows she will not impress him, and she will not say anything that might betray her daughter's secret. It is really to the audience that she turns, it is their sympathy she claims, with her ironic pointing of the insults he hurls at her:

LORD WINDERMERE: Yes, you took it – and spoiled it all last night by being found out.

MRS ERLYNNE (*with a strange smile*): You are quite right, I spoiled it all last night.

He is deaf to what Wilde calls 'the note of deep tragedy' which breaks through her usual control when she speaks of the traumatic episode of the night before:

Only once in my life have I known a mother's feelings. That was last night. They were terrible . . . they made me suffer too much. For twenty years, as you say, I have lived childless – I want to live childless still.

The germ of the play, Wilde said, (*L*,331–2), was the 'psychological idea' of a woman discovering unsuspected maternal passion, sacrificing her own interests for her child and then feeling 'This passion is too terrible. It makes me suffer too much . . . . I don't want to be a mother any more.'

Windermere cannot hear the sub-text, only the hard surface tone which in her bitterness she accentuates:

Besides, my dear Windermere, how on earth could I pose as a mother with a grown-up daughter? Margaret is twenty-one, and I have never admitted that I am more than twenty-nine, or thirty at the most. Twenty-nine when there are pink shades, thirty when there are not. So you see what difficulties it would involve.

'You fill me with horror – with absolute horror' is his imperceptive reaction.

In the third encounter, between mother and daughter, irony retreats and the characters come close to a full recognition of what the relationship between them really is, insofar as they reveal appropriate feeling for each other.

It is an emotional scene but it is protected from the extravagance that mars earlier plays by the self-critical sharp side of Mrs Erlynne's personality. She keeps a tight control, though she allows herself the painful joy of receiving her daughter's gratitude for her act of self-sacrifice, along with other smaller comforts, such as the momentary dwelling on the fact that they share the same name, 'Margaret'. Throughout the scene she is also receiving blows unwittingly dealt by Lady Windermere, as in her artless account of the grief her father suffered at his wife's 'death': 'My father – my father really died of a broken heart. His was the most ruined life I know.' The first affectionate conversation she has ever had with her own daughter brings home to Mrs Erlynne the full seriousness of what she did in the past, not in the terms of social success or failure which have preoccupied her up to now, but as a matter of 'heart' and deep personal relationships. She, as well as her daughter, has had something to learn and she has learnt. We feel the terrible weight of her realisation: it gives added poignancy to her entreaty to Lady Windermere to keep silent about what really happened in Lord Darlington's rooms:

> Don't spoil the one good thing I have done in my life by telling it to anyone. Promise me that what passed last night will remain a secret between us. You must not bring misery into your husband's life. Why spoil his love? You must not spoil it. Love is easily killed. Oh! how easily love is killed.

The audience must surely pick up here an oblique allusion to a searing moment in her dialogue with Lord Windermere, when he taunted her with what happened to her after she left her child: 'You . . . abandoned her for your lover, who abandoned you in turn.' Wilde is calling in fact for close readings of the kind for which he is not usually given credit. Under the brittle snap of the dialogue the subterranean life of feeling is delicately conveyed.

Lady Windermere keeps silent and so does Mrs Erlynne; a great relief, this, to Lord Windermere whom she left on tenter-hooks about whether or not she would reveal herself to her daughter. 'She is better than one thought her,' he says 'gravely' when he and his wife are alone at the end of the scene. Now he can continue to see his wife in the way that suits him, as an innocent little girl: 'Child, you and she belong to different worlds. Into your world evil has never entered'. She gives him a much needed lesson:

> There is the same world for all of us, and good and evil, sin and innocence, go through it hand in hand.

The Windermere idyll is resumed but Wilde does not choose to end on that note. He brings back Lord Augustus, to whom Mrs Erlynne has been giving a plausible account of the previous night. 'Arthur, she has explained everything,' he declares – and at once we see how precarious the idyll is. Husband and wife both start and Lady Windermere looks 'horribly frightened'. But all is well (this time). Lord Windermere congratulates Lord Augustus on Mrs Erlynne's acceptance of him as a husband, in cold, equivocal terms: 'Well, you are certainly marrying a very clever woman!' And Lady Windermere corrects him in the curtain-line: 'Ah, you're marrying a very good woman!' It is still naïve; as Rodney Shewan comments,[4] the concept 'good' has been totally undermined in a way she does not see. But she has learnt something about feeling: it is an advance.

In this play for the first time Wilde's satire is developed

to the full, with the aid of a wonderful chorus of comic characters. The tradition here is that of his fellow Irishmen, Sheridan and Goldsmith: we could hardly miss the echoes of *The School for Scandal* in Act 3, with its scandalmongers and discovery scene. But Wilde's satire is more stringent. The rituals of social life are subjected to a stylisation so extreme that they become disturbing: 'absurd' in the modern sense often seems the word for the comic monsters, marionettes, elegant clowns who glide through the ceremonies of the Carlton House world, like the automata in Wilde's poem, 'The Harlot's House':

> They took each other by the hand,
> And danced a stately saraband;
> Their laughter echoed thin and shrill.

The Duchess of Berwick, who leads the female chorus, is a fascinating monster: she takes her wretched daughter round with her like a mechanical doll, trained to speak only when spoken to: 'Yes, mamma,' and 'No, mamma,' are all that Lady Agatha manages to squeak. The Duchess sends her to look at photograph albums and sunsets to keep her from hearing adult conversation, and we laugh, but the laughter is complex. It is only partly against the Duchess, for she is so outrageously herself, so forthright in pursuit of her aim (to marry off Lady Agatha) that she seems to be drawing mocking attention to the manoeuvres society obliges her to perform, as when she remarks complacently: 'Dear girl! She is so fond of photographs of Switzerland. Such a pure taste, I think.' Her Olympian indifference to finer feelings is brutal but also refreshing in a curious way, like her honesty. She has no use for hypocrisy herself, though she understands very well how it works in society. When Lady Windermere announces that she will have no one in her house who is the subject of scandal and Lord Darlington teases her – 'Oh, don't say that, Lady Windermere. I should never be admitted,' – the Duchess sweeps away the refinement: 'Oh, men don't matter. With women it is different. We're good. Some of us are at least.' Her turns of phrase are at once a source of fun and a pungent reminder of her real social power. When she holds forth on Mrs Erlynne to Lady Windermere she begins with a joke and ends with an epigram, but there is all the force of the Establishment in her peremptory dismissal of this doubtful person: 'It is quite scandalous, for she is absolutely inadmissible into society. Many a woman has a past, but I am told that she has at least a dozen, and that they all fit.'

Wilde contrives to suggest from time to time that even the iron-clad Duchess is not without some tender feeling. She is not a Lady Sneerwell or a Mrs Candour, feigning sympathy in order to plant barbs the better. She seems genuinely to want to 'save' her brother, Lord Augustus, from the clutches of a woman she sees as an adventuress. The advice she gives Lady Windermere, to take her husband abroad – 'and he'll come back to you all right' – is based on her own experience as a young wife married to a compulsively promiscuous duke: '. . . on several occasions after I was first married, I had to pretend to be very ill, and was obliged to drink the most unpleasant mineral waters, merely to get Berwick out of town. He was so extremely susceptible.' Unlike Lord Windermere, she adds drily, her duke never gave away large sums of money to anybody: 'He is far too high-principled for that!' Good jokes but they give way, unexpectedly, to a softer note, when the young wife miserably says, 'Windermere and I married for love,' and the Duchess replies, surely not without sadness, 'Yes, we begin like that.'

This ability to vary the mode and the mood, even when working with caricatures, is one of Wilde's great and under-estimated achievements. We see it again in the second act, when in the more public scene of the ball, he has a much larger collection of comic characters to handle. It is the final set of the 'game of marriage' the Duchess is playing on behalf of her 'little chatterbox'. Lady Agatha says 'Yes' (Does she in habit add 'Mamma', we wonder!) to Mr Hopper, the comically-named Australian who scores his own small triumph by returning the ball in a rally with the Duchess at her most sublimely patronising: 'Do you know, Mr Hopper, dear Agatha and I are so interested in Australia. It must be so pretty with all the dear little kangaroos flying about. Agatha has found it on the map. What a curious shape it is! Just like a large packing case. However, it is a very young country, isn't it?' 'Wasn't it made at the same time as the others, Duchess?', he returns, with an unruffled promptness which suggests that this is one 'outsider' who will hold his own in the disdainful parish of St James. It is a money bargain that is being struck, as the Duchess makes wickedly clear: 'Ah! We know your value, Mr Hopper. We wish there were more like you. It would make life so much easier.' With still more outrageous candour she utters her final comment before sailing out with Lady Agatha in tow, the business concluded: 'Love – well, not love at first sight, but love at the end of the season, which is so much more satisfactory.' It is delightfully droll; yet unmistakably the same area of country which Shaw makes the subject for blistering, passionate attack on the 'selling' of young girls in *Mrs Warren's Profession*.

In the background of the Duchess' campaign is a comic chorus devoted to gossip, scandal, and the discreet conduct of extra-marital liaisons. It is these people, in the mass, who decide the fate of the less discreet or more sensitive and passionate characters. Like the infatuated beings in *Salomé*, all are intently watching each other: 'I really must have a good stare at her', says Lady Plymdale, greedily observing Mrs Erlynne. 'That woman' is the chief focus of attention as she winds her way in among the women ('I am afraid of the women . . . the men I can always manage,' she tells Lord Windermere). Both groups are uneasy; the women jealous, the men alarmed that their attentions to Mrs Erlynne may be found out. Wilde draws much comedy from this unease. There are amusing contradictions and double takes, as when Lady Plymdale having been assured by Dumby that he has hardly even heard of Mrs Erlynne, is greeted warmly by that lady: 'Ah, Mr Dumby, how are you? I am so sorry I have been out the last three times you have called.' 'What an absolute brute you are,' is Lady Plymdale's first reaction, but when she has taken her 'good stare' and had time to reflect, she instructs Dumby to accept Mrs Erlynne's lunch invitation and take Lady Plymdale's husband with him: '. . . This woman's just the thing for him. He'll dance attendance upon her as long as she lets him, and won't bother me. I assure you, women of that kind are most useful. They form the basis of other people's marriages.' Lady Plymdale is in the end a menacing rather than a comic figure, a reminder that society protects the cold-hearted who know how to take their pleasure within the conventions, having their cake and eating it.

In the third act the perspective changes and events are seen from the viewpoint of an all-male chorus. The party of gentlemen in Lord Darlington's room, like their forebears in Restoration comedy, amuse themselves with banter and gossip about women, sharpening their wits on their more naïve fellows. Lord Augustus is their butt – yet it is he who engages our sympathy. It is a touching moment when he holds out against their cynical view of Mrs Erlynne: 'You want to make her out a wicked woman! She is not.' The play is to show that he is right, but they cannot see it; for all their sophistication, they are stupidly trapped in their prejudices about 'good' and 'bad' women. 'Mrs Erlynne has a future before her,' says Lord Augustus, drawing from Dumby the riposte, 'Mrs Erlynne has a past before her.' A witty reply which gets a laugh but is also a reminder of something depressing about this society: the idea of the 'woman with a past' has become a crippling abstraction. Lord Augustus is closer to the facts of life when he says quite simply: 'I prefer women with a past. They're always so demmed amusing to talk to.'

The scene ends with a verbal fireworks display which contains some of Wilde's most celebrated epigrams (including transfers from *Vera*):

> LORD DARLINGTON: You always amuse me, Cecil. You talk as if you were a man of experience.
>
> CECIL GRAHAM: I am.
>
> LORD DARLINGTON: You are far too young!
>
> CECIL GRAHAM: That is a great error. Experience is a question of instinct about life. I have got it. Tuppy hasn't. Experience is the name Tuppy gives to his mistakes. That is all.
>
> DUMBY: Experience is the name everyone gives to their mistakes.

Like so many of Wilde's scintillating passages, however, this is not just fireworks. 'Instinct about life' is the serious question all have to settle in the play: whether to live in the cynical 'heartless' mode, where conventional ideas about women suffice, or to go for real experience, risking mistakes but perhaps emerging with truer values. It is important for directors and actors to recognise the delicate balance of fun and biting satire, for when the comedy gives way to melodrama with the discovery of the fan, it should not seem a leap into a quite alien mode, but rather a continuation in more emotional vein of what has been explored up to then through wit.

Stylisation of speech is Wilde's most important means of lifting a potentially banal action into the realm of art. He uses highly patterned sentences, repetition, rhythmic cadences, to create strong, secular rituals, as in the ball scene of Act 2:

> DUMBY: Good evening, Lady Stutfield. I suppose this will be the last ball of the season?
>
> LADY STUTFIELD: I suppose so, Mr Dumby. It's been a delightful season, hasn't it?
>
> DUMBY: Quite delightful! Good evening, Duchess. I suppose this will be the last ball of the season?
>
> DUCHESS OF BERWICK: I suppose so, Mr Dumby. It has been a very dull season, hasn't it?
>
> DUMBY: Dreadfully dull! Dreadfully dull!

Rhythm rules. Wilde told Alexander while in the early stages of writing that he was having difficulty in getting his people 'real'. Evidently he heard the cadences, the epigrams, the rounded turns of phrase and had to adjust them to characters who at first may have been to him no more than voices. His great achievement was to fill out the voices so as to make them utterly believable as people. The 'last ball' sequence can be played, as I have seen it done, in masks, with taped voices, as a near-Expressionist ritual. But it also works perfectly in a more realistic treatment.

There are two rhythms in *Lady Windermere's Fan*, one

light, one heavy. The old melodrama rhythm with its operatic quality comes up again here, as in the earlier plays, whenever the emotions thicken, and feeling forces its way through the smooth and decorous façade. The transitions are clearly predictable. When Mrs Erlynne discovers the letter her daughter has written to Lord Darlington, rhythm and tone change instantly from her previously cool style to: 'What can I do? I feel a passion awakening within me that I never felt before.' And when she makes her tremendous appeal to Lady Windermere to return to her husband and her child, all the operatic stops are pulled out:

> Go back, Lady Windermere, to the husband who loves you, whom you love. You have a child, Lady Windermere. Go back to that child who even now, in pain or in joy, may be calling to you. . . . Back to your house, Lady Windermere – your husband loves you! He has never swerved for a moment from the love he bears you. But even if he had a thousand loves, you must stay with your child. If he was harsh to you, you must stay with your child. If he ill-treated you, you must stay with your child. If he abandoned you, your place is with your child.

Tremolo fiddles may seem called for at this point: it is certainly the rhythm of the melodrama stage. Yet, with customary skill, Wilde adjusts that rhythm which so haunted him to the psychological needs of the characters. The heavy beat and relentless repetition of 'Stay with your child' convey well the impression of a mind dominated by a passionate idea. In speaking of Lady Windermere's child Mrs Erlynne is also thinking of Lady Windermere as her own child whom she abandoned. Now she has the opportunity to work for that child, to save her, and she is taking it to the full, winning her reward when Lady Windermere holds out her hands 'helplessly, as a child', saying 'Take me home', as if she had understood that she is appealing to her mother. Wilde's mastery of these so different rhythms – melodrama, high comedy, naturalism – is a crucial factor in the stylisation of his 'real life' material.

Stylisation of scene and décor, though less obvious, is also important. The earlier reviewers were struck by the lifelike appearance of Alexander's settings, but Wilde's stage directions really call for a rather bare stage; it is defined in terms of 'spaces' with a few focal points like the bureau which Lady Windermere rifles and the curtain across the window in Lord Darlington's rooms. Some of these spaces acquire symbolic overtones. The terrace, for instance, becomes associated with sexual encounters and 'the game of marriage' in a way which at first seems no more than conventional – where else to go for proposals and flirtations? – but eventually makes it a rather ominous place. 'The air is fresh there,' says the Duchess, fanning herself. But it is not so very fresh: the meetings of the sexes that occur there are equivocal or even sordid. It is on the terrace that the marriage bargain between Lady Agatha and rich Mr Hopper is concluded and it is to the terrace that Mrs Erlynne takes Lord Windermere to persuade him to make a settlement on her and improve her chances with Lord Augustus. The sight of her husband disappearing onto the terrace with her seeming rival is what decides Lady Windermere that they really are engaged in a liaison and leads her to take up Lord Darlington's offer.

Other important visual effects are provided by costume, tableaux and significant groupings of characters. One of the most striking occurs in the scene when Mrs Erlynne is discovered in Lord Darlington's room. Wilde contrives a deliberate and arresting contrast between the men in their evening suits, all gathered together at one side of the stage, and the one woman, Mrs Erlynne, appearing from the inner room at the other side, to freeze them all in attitudes of shock and horror. Contemporary reviews were apt to be illustrated by photographs of this scene which clearly shows its symbolism even out of context; an interesting proof of Wilde's visual sense. Wilde found the black and white of men's evening wear monotonous and rather dispiriting, though he also thought that black could provide a useful ground for the colours of women's dresses in a stage scene. Here he makes artful use of sartorial monotony to suggest a masculine uniform from which no slight variation is allowed. The tailcoats and stiff shirts form a solid mass of black and white, a formidable opposition to the woman who seems especially vulnerable in her isolation and the fragility of her evening dress, which in the style of the 1890s reveals a good deal of nakedness. This symbolic grouping is a silent testimony to the unfair tipping of society's scales against women.

Among the objects which acquire special visual significance, the most important is the fan. Wilde takes this little object through his plot with the adroitness of Goldoni (in *The Fan*). It is a love token, a birthday gift from Lord Windermere, which becomes a weapon of hate when Lady Windermere threatens to strike Mrs Erlynne in the face with it if her husband insists on bringing to the ball the woman gossip makes his mistress. It is a measure of Wilde's delicacy of feeling that he found this imagined situation extremely painful: he was determined to conceal the woman's relationship from the audience until much later in the play because he thought they would not be able to bear, any more than he could, the idea of a daughter unwittingly threatening to strike her own mother in the face. He maintained the secrecy until after the traumatic moment.

In the ball scene Lady Windermere ostentatiously entrusts the fan to Lord Darlington, tormenting her husband with terrible possibilities: 'A useful thing, a fan, is it not?' We wait in suspense as she faces Mrs Erlynne; if she were to carry out her threat, it would in this context be an act of violence comparable to the dagger thrusts of earlier plays. She does not, but lets the fan fall on the floor, to have it restored to her by Lord Darlington; when she flies to his rooms it goes with her, to be found by the gossiping men when she forgets it in her panicky retreat behind the curtain. The little white object in the context of the bachelor's rooms is no longer harmless but signifies a forbidden intimacy which excites them all – at first to a slightly salacious mirth (close to the genial voyeurism of Sheridan's screen scene), then to a dark, threatening mood when Lord Windermere recognises the fan as his wife's. Tragedy is close at this moment, for he is not the man to believe in her innocence, should she be revealed: their life together would collapse. It is the sense of this that gives importance, even grandeur to the finale when Mrs Erlynne steps forward and assumes responsibility for the fan. Nothing could better demonstrate Wilde's mastery of his new mode of stylised naturalism. No rhetoric is needed, no sensationalism. A fashionable woman speaks a few conventional words about a trivial object: 'I am afraid I took your wife's fan in mistake for my own, when I was leaving your house tonight. I am so sorry.' But what a bombshell: we feel the shock waves; then the curtain falls, leaving us to wonder whether the little fan has really brought the house down.

By the final act the fan has become so loaded with significance that when Parker brings it on a tray with a message from Mrs Erlynne, it is almost like the presentation of the head on the silver charger to Salomé. The fan does have that kind of horrific meaning for Windermere: it is 'soiled' by its association with Mrs Erlynne and, we might guess, by the unworthy thoughts he allowed himself to entertain for a moment about his wife. In his loathing of the fan he has turned away from the fuller experience of the human heart that is in the end associated with the fragile object. For in the touching final scene between mother and daughter the fine feeling that has been wrung from the pain and anxiety is mutely symbolised in the gift from daughter to mother of the 'wonderful fan' which has the name they share inscribed upon it. Lady Windermere will never know that Mrs Erlynne is her mother, but for her, unconsciously perhaps, while for Mrs Erlynne so consciously, the transference of the fan represents a feminine communion which has the quality of their true relationship.

It is Mrs Erlynne who moves the action to an ending which if not totally happy is at any rate an escape from tragedy. It is she too who in the final act provides a witty perspective on the emotionalism of a scene bereft of its comic characters. She is the major wit of the play and her irony provides the necessary bulwark against the sentimentality and hysteria which continually threaten to engulf the characters. When Windermere taunts her with having been abandoned by her lover, her ironical riposte – 'Do you count that to his credit, Lord Windermere – or to mine?' – preserves her self-respect and provides a bitterly amused gloss on the dubious morals of the society which makes the woman the scapegoat for the frailty of the male.

Her wit is steelier than Lord Darlington's and does not collapse as his does under the pressure of passion. We can tell that there is a world of hard lessons behind her sharp summing up of people and opportunities. She has been damaged by her experience: Wilde's treatment of her is entirely realistic. She has a calculating side and can play the hypocrite; her easy assumption that she can always manage the men has a touch of vulgarity and reminds us that the phrase 'woman with a past' can be applied to her in the full *boulevard* sense. But her sensitivity is still there under the carapace of hard wit.

Wit and feeling come together indeed when she uses her masterful ability to save her daughter. Her discovery that a mother's feelings are 'terrible', her suffering and her self-sacrifice call up thoughts of that other clever, self-sacrificing mother, Ibsen's Mrs Alving. Wilde seems to have had in mind one of the most telling moments in *Ghosts*, when Mrs Alving sees Oswald and Regina kissing and cries 'Ghosts!' at the horrific image of the past repeating itself. Just so Mrs Erlynne shudders when she reads her daughter's letter telling Lord Darlington that she will come to him: 'No, no! It would be impossible! Life doesn't repeat its tragedies like that! . . . The same words that twenty years ago I wrote to her father! And how bitterly I have been punished for it. No; my punishment, my real punishment is tonight, is now!' Like Mrs Alving, Mrs Erlynne learns something about herself from being forced to relive the painful experience of the past. In the year *Lady Windermere's Fan* was written, Wilde, as we have seen, was extremely enthusiastic about Elizabeth Robins' performance as Hedda Gabler. Brack's famous phrase 'People don't do such things' is surely recalled in Mrs Erlynne's mocking 'I suppose, Windermere, you would like me to retire into a convent, or become a hospital nurse. . . . That is stupid of you, Arthur; in real life we don't do such things.' Mrs Erlynne is no Hedda – she openly ran away with her lover, and we cannot imagine her killing herself – but she is in a similarly ironical and critical relationship to a society obsessed with surface respectability, yet condoning discreet sexual peccadilloes like those of a Lady Plymdale or a Judge Brack. In Wilde's play as in Ibsen's there is an overwhelming sense of a suppressed or unacknowledged inner life coming through the barbed, elliptical dialogue. Perhaps her blackest moment is in Lord Darlington's rooms when she realises for the first time that she is suspected by her daughter of being Windermere's mistress. She sees that the life she has led is what feeds the suspicion: it is also the reason why she cannot tell her daughter the truth, but when Lady Windermere asks 'What have I to do with you?' must reply 'Nothing'. She says it 'humbly': her character, we see, has been purged and refined by the painful maternal love she comes to feel. This too is the stuff of tragedy.

Yet in other ways the stern demands of tragedy are refused. Lady Windermere is never to know the truth: Mrs Erlynne will keep it from her, as Mrs Alving kept the truth about his disreputable father from Oswald. In *Ghosts* that suppression is shown to have been a terrible mistake. In his play, Wilde seems to suggest it is necessary; that is Mrs Erlynne's view at least. She tells her daughter, when urging her to return to her husband, that she has not the strength of character for what she proposes to do: 'You haven't got the kind of brains that enable a woman to get back. You have neither the wit nor the courage.' When Windermere in the final scene decides that after all he should tell his wife the truth, Mrs Erlynne is violent in her resistance: 'If you do, I will make my name so infamous that it will mar every moment of her life. . . . There is no degradation I will not sink to, no pit of shame I will not enter.' She means at all costs to preserve the false image, the dead mother, of whom the daughter says at the end: 'We all

1a. Setting designed by Charles Ricketts for *Salomé* and used for the production at King's Hall, Covent Garden, 1906.

1b. Rex Whistler's design for the Octagon Room, Act 1 of *An Ideal Husband*.

2a. Charles Ricketts' costume design for the Young Syrian, *Salomé*. Replica of the lost original design for the Tokyo production, 1919.

2b. Gustav Moreau's *The Apparition* (The dance of Salomé).

3. *Salomé* (Lindsay Kemp) holding Jokanaan. Lindsay Kemp's production of *Salomé*, Round House, 1977.

4. Miss Marion Terry as Mrs. Erlynne in *Lady Windermere's Fan*, St. James' Theatre, 1892.

5a. Lord Darlington & Company. Scene from Act III of *Lady Windermere's Fan*, St. James' Theatre, 1892.

5b. Scene from Act III of *A Woman of No Importance* (Stop, Gerald, he is your father!), 1893.

6b. Caricature of John Gielgud as John Worthing in *The Importance of Being Earnest*, Globe, 1940.

6a. George Alexander as John Worthing in Act II of *The Importance of Being Earnest*, St. James' Theatre, 1895.

7. John Gielgud as John Worthing, Gwen Frangeon-Davies as Gwendolen and Edith Evans as Lady Bracknell in Act I of *The Importance of Being Earnest*, Globe Theatre, 1939/40.

8a. Anna Massey as Miss Prism, Martin Jarvis as John Worthing and Judi Dench as Lady Bracknell in *The Importance of Being Earnest*, The National Theatre, 1982.

8b. Martin Jarvis as John Worthing, Zoë Wanamaker as Gwendolen Fairfax, Elizabeth Garvie as Cecily Cardew and Nigel Havers as Algernon Moncrieff in *The Importance of Being Earnest*, The National Theatre, 1982.

have ideals in life. At least we all should have. Mine is my mother.' It is hard for the living mother: she and her daughter have become so close emotionally, she must be tempted to tell her the truth. She knows too that 'Ideals are dangerous things. Realities are better. They wound, but they're better.' But when she hears Lady Windermere say 'If I lost my ideals, I should lose everything,' she sees that it will not do. Instead she asks a sad question about the past: 'Did your father often speak to you of your mother?' And then she turns away from the sadness, leaving Lady Windermere with her illusions.

Is it a sentimental evasion? Perhaps, but it is rooted in realistic assessment of character, for Mrs Erlynne is not destined for tragedy: she is a survivor, as she demonstrates by capturing Lord Augustus after all, and departing with him for the Continent in a triumph of a kind. The wheel has come full circle, the puritan has learnt her lesson, and the women share a secret which is shown to be more important than the secret of Mrs Erlynne's past, for it is to do with love and self-sacrifice, the supreme good in Wilde's morality. Lord Augustus, like Lady Windermere, is deceived, but for his own good: no doubt he is so easily satisfied with Mrs Erlynne's 'explanations' because he wants to be. It is a happy ending for him to be taken in hand by her: she may be descended from the erring ladies of Sardou and the *boulevard* theatre (the *Pall Mall* reviewer at the first night saw the play as no more than a half-hearted treatment of the subject handled by Dumas fils in *Françillon*). But Wilde has made of her something quite new. It is good to know that she was played by Marion Terry, the first Mrs Erlynne, 'with incomparable grace and spirit', for through this character Wilde made his first telling criticism of the strange, hypocritical society which created the concept of the 'woman with a past'.

6
'A Woman of No Importance'

First performed 19 April 1893, Haymarket Theatre.
Published 1893.

A Woman of No Importance followed fast on the heels of
Lady Windermere's Fan and has many obvious links with
its predecessor, beginning with the title page description 'A
new and original play of modern life'. There is the same
classical unity of a twenty-four-hour time span, the same
type of rich and privileged *dramatis personae*, the same
well-worn situation of the 'woman with a past'. There is
wit in abundance, indeed as some critics have thought, in
over-abundance, and there is melodrama of which the
same might be said. Mrs Bernard Beere (who was to have
played Vera) took the arduous part of Mrs Arbuthnot and
Beerbohm Tree played Lord Illingworth, a part tailor-
made for him. It was another fashionable play with
fashionable actors given for a fashionable audience.

'A Woman of No Importance'

But though the elements are so similar the mixture is very different: some quite new things are done. Wilde himself drew attention to one distinctive aspect in a letter of February 1893 to an actor who was hoping for a part: 'In my new play there are very few men's parts – it is a woman's play.' In every way this is true. It is a 'woman's play' in sympathy with women from the implications of its ironic title to the ending where that title is overturned and becomes 'A man of no importance'. It was also new, as Wilde declared with considerable pride, that in his first act 'there was absolutely no action at all. It was a perfect act.'[1] For modern audiences the notion has a resonance it could not have had for Wilde's contemporaries: they were inclined to see the static conversational structure of the first act as a self-indulgent arrangement for witty talk. We have been taught, however, by *Waiting for Godot* that stasis where we expect dynamic movement can create subtle dramatic tension and interest. Beckett's Estragon and Vladimir amusing themselves with *louche* routines are at a far remove from Wilde's lords and ladies chatting on the lawn at Hunstanton, yet their activities are not dissimilar. Wilde's characters too are busily occupied in filling in the time, getting through the long spaces of an ordinary afternoon, creating a stage on which their existence will have more point, with the aid of wit and story-telling. At a deep level – which most of them do not consciously recognise (Lord Illingworth and Mrs Allonby are the brilliant exceptions: W. B. Yeats observed that they had a kind of 'wisdom') – they are engaged in the existential process which Wilde believed was the purpose of life. Through the immensely long conversation piece of the first act they are revealing in their own way the patterns of their inner life.

The world of Illingworth, Mrs Allonby and even Lady

Hunstanton, is a subtle one, far indeed, one might think, from the simple, lurid world of melodrama. Yet the conventions of melodrama, the clear-cut, Old Testament morality, the hard and fast rules, are powerful here, as in *Lady Windermere's Fan*. In this play Wilde is especially interested in the curious relationship between the two worlds. The sophisticated hedonists are given as much room as the leading figures in the melodrama: the 'woman with a past', her illegitimate son, her unregenerate seducer and the young puritan, 'a sort of alarum of morality who rings at intervals', as a contemporary reviewer put it.[2]

From the start we are aware that a subterranean life of emotion runs underneath the dialogue; in the melodramatic passages it breaks through to the surface, but it can be sensed even in the opening talk before tea, on Lady Hunstanton's lawn. It is a Jamesian scene; an English country house party where the conversation is mannered and oblique, hidden sexual relationships are hinted at and there is a fascinating gap between what is said and what might be meant. There is too a quite Jamesian opposition between the English style, elegant but morally suspect, and the style of the young American visitor, tactless, emotionally earnest and alarmingly direct. James might not have approved the comparison, for he disliked Wilde's comedies (especially *An Ideal Husband*), yet we can hardly escape it: American allusions are everywhere in the play, including the joke about 'dry goods' ('What are American dry goods? American novels.'). And in his own terms, which means, always, a high degree of comic stylisation, Wilde explores the psychology of his country house characters, with an attention to fine betraying detail which in 1892 could only be matched in the novels of James. Natural expression of feeling is suspect in this society, as we learn when Hester, in her uninhibited American way, talks candidly of her liking for Gerald and dislike for Mrs Allonby, and is snubbed by Lady Caroline: 'Mrs Allonby is very well born. She is a niece of Lord Brancaster's.'

Disguises must be worn. Lady Hunstanton's absent-mindedness, for instance (Lord Illingworth tells her it is one of her most fascinating qualities), allows her to take part in gossip and scandalmongering without forfeiting goodwill. To the discussion of the interesting question, why Lord Illingworth never married, she contributes a quite surrealist 'memory': Lady Kelso was a candidate, 'But I believe he said her family was too large. Or was it her feet? I forget which.' As played by Rose Leclerq, she came over to contemporary reviewers as a very rounded personality ('glib, good-natured, irresponsible, delight-fully evasive'). It is *The School for Scandal* again, and again Wilde draws different tunes from the old notes. As other characters drift on to the lawn – elegant, waspish Mrs Allonby, effusive Lady Stutfield with her trademark of 'very very' and 'quite quite' – we begin to realise that the seemingly inconsequential talk allows release for feelings which would be unacceptable in more emotional form; mannerism is both a form of control and a subtle means of letting go. It is something the frank American girl cannot understand at all – any more than have some of Wilde's critics.

From time to time, in this infinitely leisurely first act, we are given snatches of 'plot'. Gerald arrives, full of his good fortune at being offered a post as secretary by Lord Illingworth: we see that Hester and he are drawn to each other, are told that Gerald's mother, much admired by Lady Hunstanton for her 'saintly' reclusive life, may join the house party that evening, and guess that some kind of trouble over Gerald is looming. But these moments are no more, indeed are a good deal less important in the total effect than the 'trivia' of the tea-table conversation.

All the voices are idiosyncratic. We could not mistake Lady Caroline's booming notes for the ironical, risqué jokes of Mrs Allonby, or confuse that lady's smooth tone with the repetitive chirpings of her fellow flirt, Lady Stutfield. 'Minor' and 'major' are meaningless terms for the characters of the first act. Mrs Allonby is the first in a new line of women characters, a female dandy, who uses her wit with aplomb and ruthlessness to make life more amusing for herself. That 'double standard' which was the source of so much misery in *Lady Windermere's Fan* is to her no more than an extra titillation in the sexual game. She enjoys playing with fire: as she tells Lady Caroline 'It is the people who don't know how to play with it who get burned up.' ('Very, very helpful,' murmurs silly Lady Stutfield.) And she responds to the latter's comment that 'The world was made for men and not for women,' with the impudently amoral 'Oh, don't say that, Lady Stutfield. We have a much better time than they have. There are far more things forbidden to us than are forbidden to them.' Her hearers exclaim at her risky remarks but it is evident that they are not really shocked. The long-drawn-out, frivolous dialogue among the women builds up an impression of a bold, self-willed mental life only just below the surface of the decorous front the ladies present to the world. They understand Mrs Allonby too well not to have something in common with her, though perhaps they would not go so far in playing with fire as she does (Lady Stutfield, one suspects, may say less and go further).

The sense of secret pleasure and mockery in these feminine conversations provides a sardonic gloss on the conventional and abstract idea of women's place in society which is expressed by the earnest politician, Mr Kelvil. In this sophisticated world he appears a perfect booby who is certainly bringing his great campaign for 'Purity' ('The one subject of really national importance') to the wrong market. 'Women are always on the side of morality, public and private,' he pompously proclaims, drawing from Lady Stutfield the absurd 'It is so very, very gratifying to hear you say that,' and from Lady Hunstanton a revealing leap of thought to a man who is much in the minds of all the ladies, Lord Illingworth. Lady Stutfield takes up her reference to him with relish. 'The world says that Lord Illingworth is very, very wicked,' and pat on cue Lord Illingworth appears, placing himself and his philosophy with entire accuracy: 'But what world says that, Lady Stutfield? It must be the next world. This world and I are on excellent terms.'

The scene that follows demonstrates the truth of that remark. Lord Illingworth fascinates by his mastery of the worldly world, the sense he gives of being so at ease in it that he need not wear much in the way of disguise or pretend to feelings he does not really have. Always there is a hint of steely intellectual life under the witticisms he scatters with an air of languor ('artistic quietude' was one reviewer's phrase for Tree's performance). He has a devastating gift for summing up a whole way of life in an epigram, as in his description of the fox-hunting class as 'the unspeakable in full pursuit of the uneatable,' or in his dry comments on American women. 'Why can't they stay in their own country?' says Lady Caroline fretfully, once the vexing American girl is off the stage, 'They are always telling us it is the paradise of women.' 'It is, Lady Caroline,' he assures her. 'That is why, like Eve, they are so extremely anxious to get out of it.' The rally ends with panache:

MRS ALLONBY: They say, Lady Hunstanton, that when good Americans die they go to Paris.

LADY HUNSTANTON: Indeed? And when bad Americans die, where do they go to?

LORD ILLINGWORTH: Oh, they go to America.

But it is not random: American style, American morals will not be a joking matter later on. Behind the seemingly light-hearted fun is the suggestion of a hostile English response to a threat already anticipated. Similarly, when politics come into the conversation through the sententious Mr Kelvil, Lord Illingworth's cynicism allows Wilde to express some revolutionary questioning of the status quo:

KELVIL: You cannot deny that the House of Commons has always shown great sympathy with the sufferings of the poor.

LORD ILLINGWORTH: That is its special vice. That is the special vice of the age. One should sympathise with the joy, the beauty, the colour of life. The less said about life's sores the better, Mr Kelvil.

KELVIL: Still our East End is a very important problem.

LORD ILLINGWORTH: Quite so. It is the problem of slavery. And we are trying to solve it by amusing the slaves.

Mrs Allonby is Lord Illingworth's match, as we see when she makes her audacious exit with him, blandly explaining that she is going 'just as far as the conservatory. Lord Illingworth told me this morning that there was an orchid there as beautiful as the seven deadly sins.' Lady Hunstanton restores decorum: 'My dear, I hope there is nothing of the kind. I will certainly speak to the gardener.' She will not let anyone go too far, though neither will she admit that Mrs Allonby does this. 'She lets her clever tongue run away with her,' she says placatingly to Lady Caroline (who replies, implacably, 'Is that the only thing, Jane, Mrs Allonby allows to run away with her?'). Wilde evidently relished the scope the lack of 'plot' gave him to develop these 'rich evasions' in the sub-text of English conversation, using the English actors' special gift for playing 'between the lines'. Some early critics were baffled. Even C. E. Montague found himself at sea: '. . . for a long time after the rise of the curtain one wondered, Would there be a play at all? There was talking, not drama.'[3] Max Beerbohm was one of the very few (then or later) to recognise that the 'talking' *was* drama. He saw that in this play Wilde 'allowed the psychological idea to work itself out almost unmolested, and the play was, in my opinion, by far the most truly dramatic of his plays.'[4]

Wilde does something in this subtle conversation piece which had been attempted before in English comedy only by Congreve. He opened the way for the Shaw of *Getting Married*, Granville Barker, and the many playwrights since who have explored through long drawn-out, seemingly casual talk the social and psychic complexity of personal relationships. When the group dissolves and Mrs Allonby is left alone with Lord Illingworth, to conduct an ambiguous flirtation, they talk entirely in code. She will always like him, she says, because he has never made love to her. He replies that he has never done anything else. 'Really?' she says, 'I have not noticed it.' 'How unfortunate!' he returns. 'It might have been a tragedy for both of us.' We must provide our own translation of this guarded exchange. Wilde points up its equivocal nature through a sharp contrast with the artless openness of the young lovers, Hester and Gerald, who momentarily interrupt their elders' fencing match, irritating Mrs

Allonby intensely with their candour and sincerity. 'She told me yesterday, and in quite a loud voice too, that she was only eighteen. It was most annoying.' It is a joke with a sting, against herself in an obvious way; less obviously, it carries implications for her relationship with Lord Illingworth. A curious voyeurism creeps in when she deliberately provokes him to think about 'Puritan' women, and he responds with a complacent: 'Do you know, I don't believe in the existence of Puritan women? I don't think there is a woman in the world who would not be a little flattered if one made love to her!' She fastens on the idea, encourages him to test it by kissing Hester and speculates with cold voyeuristic interest on how the girl would be likely to react: would she marry him or strike him in the face with her glove? The thought of the violent act clearly excites them both (and seems to have excited Wilde, for it is the second time he has used the idea of a face slap). These are lovers who need such stimuli, it seems; their pleasures are arcane.

As they prepare to leave for the 'simple pleasures' (Mrs Allonby's term) of tea with the company in the yellow drawing-room, time is momentarily arrested: Lord Illingworth glimpses the hand-writing on the letter left lying by Lady Hunstanton and is at once back in the past, recognising the hand 'of a woman I used to know years ago'. He pushes the memory away with the dismissive 'Oh! no one. A woman of no importance,' but it has been enough to indicate the stirring in him of an emotion that may upset the elegant equilibrium of his hedonistic life. The act ends on a note of delicate suggestiveness; as the two go into the house via the terrace they pause for a moment and 'smile at each other'. It is a telling moment of silent communication, such as we associate with Chekhov or Pinter more commonly than with Wilde.

There are many such in the unexpected sub-text of this play.

The second act opens with the emphasis even more firmly on women and their only half-hidden private lives. It is the moment after dinner when the ladies have withdrawn to the drawing-room, having left the men to their port and masculine conversation. No more than a familiar social convention, this, for the stalls audience at the St James's Theatre, but in Wilde's hands the piece of commonplace reality is made to show its true nature as one of the strange rituals by which this society maintains the separateness of the men's world and covertly endorses the assumption that more freedom is allowed to them than to women.

There is an ironic aspect to the rite which Wilde especially delights to show. The gentlemen's freedom is decidedly limited: half an hour after dinner is all they are allowed by the ladies in the way of respite from decorum and refined hypocrisy. Mrs Allonby typically draws attention to the irony in her flippant professions of relief at having got rid of the men for a little: 'The annoying thing is that the wretches can be perfectly happy without us. That is why I think it is every woman's duty never to leave them alone for a single moment, except during this short breathing space after dinner; without which, I believe, we poor women would be absolutely worn to shadows.' Women's perpetual task is to keep men up to the mark. 'They are always trying to escape from us,' she says, a candid joke that draws from Lady Stutfield a stereotyped 'feminine' reaction – 'Men are so very, very heartless. They know their power and use it,' – and from Lady Caroline a brusque dismissal of the stuff and nonsense that is being talked. She knows that all that is required is 'to keep men in their proper place'.

Mrs Allonby, played first by Lady Tree 'with perfect point', is the solo virtuoso in the conversational concerto. She allows herself a freedom in talking about her husband which takes her to the very edge of what is permissible, even in the relaxed atmosphere of the all-female gathering. She mocks his strong chin, his lack of conversation and – right on the edge now – his sexual inadequacy, for this is surely what lies behind her extravagant joke about her disappointment when she found out after marriage that he had spoken the truth (though she had not believed him) when he swore that he had never loved anyone before her. 'And that sort of thing always makes a man so absolutely uninteresting,' she concludes, drawing from Lady Hunstanton a presumably rather shocked 'My dear!'. *The Importance of Being Earnest* can be sensed drawing nearer during this splendid passage. The disappointing husband is Ernest by name as well as, evidently, by nature: the great joke has almost taken shape.

Invited by Lady Stutfield to describe her concept of the Ideal Husband, Mrs Allonby dismisses the whole idea of marriage: 'The Ideal Husband? There couldn't be such a thing. The institution is wrong.' Then, like a latter-day Millamant, she lays out the 'provisos' which would make a relationship with a man endurable:

> . . . he should be always ready to have a perfectly terrible scene, whenever we want one, and to become miserable, absolutely miserable, at a moment's notice . . . and send one little notes every half hour by private hansom, and dine quite alone at the club, so that everyone should know how unhappy he was.

Finally, when he has been sufficiently chastened, 'it becomes a woman's duty to forgive, and one can do it all over again from the beginning, with variations.' 'How clever you are, my dear!' says Lady Hunstanton, 'You never mean a single word you say.' The remark draws attention to the cover, clever indeed, under which Mrs Allonby goes her own way and takes her pleasure. No one is ever sure how serious she is or what the nature of her pleasure may be. 'Infinite expectation' is to be the Ideal Man's reward – so she says! But whether or not she takes lovers, it is clear that she will never 'surrender' herself. She is the coolest of customers and society is therefore her oyster.

Having given his wordly women their head, Wilde confronts them with their antithesis, the young American puritan, maintaining a subtle balance of sympathy in the clash that develops between the experienced ladies and the naïve, idealistic girl who is shocked by what to them is commonplace talk. She holds forth on the moral superiority of America with a raw patriotic enthusiasm which invites the ironic responses it predictably draws from the ladies, for she is certainly very crude. When she compares decadent English society with 'a leper in purple', a 'dead thing smeared with gold', the throbbing style can hardly be to our taste. Yet though too easily carried away, she seems right when she castigates the shallow, self-indulgent nature of the life these people lead, their lack of care for 'the unseen beauty of life, the unseen beauty of a higher life'.

Wilde means to make quite sure that we do from time to time see his charmingly witty people in that sterner light. Hester's radical sentiments are just those he proclaimed as his own in the earlier plays. The mention of Lord Henry Weston by Lady Hunstanton draws from her a denunciation quite in the style of *Vera*: 'A man with a hideous smile and a hideous past. He is asked everywhere.

No dinner party is complete without him. What of those whose ruin is due to him? They are outcasts. They are nameless.' Strong echoes here from Hawthorne's *The Scarlet Letter*. A dramatisation of the novel had been performed in London a few years before: Wilde clearly expected his audience to pick up his oblique allusions to that rabid Puritanism of New England.[5] Hester's name looks to Hester Prynne, Hawthorne's heroine, who was forced to stand in public carrying her illegitimate child and wearing the letter 'A' (for adulteress) embroidered on her dress. It is probably no accident that Mrs Arbuthnot's name begins with A. 'One name is as good as another, when one has no right to any name,' she says bitterly to her seducer when he asks her on their first meeting 'Why Arbuthnot?'.

While the young puritan holds forth, a ghost enters the company. Mrs Arbuthnot has crept noiselessly in from the terrace. Cloaked, a lace veil over her head, she stands silently overhearing Hester's denunciation of sinners. The men come back into the room and Lord Illingworth is brought over to be introduced to Gerald's mother; still in the cynical mood induced by *badinage* with Mrs Allonby, he expects to be bored and instead receives a shock.

We are emphatically not given a melodramatic encounter: indeed, the scene between them when they are left alone together is a new kind of triumph for Wilde in low-key naturalism. Archer perceptively singled it out as 'the most virile and intelligent' dramatic writing of the day. Illingworth sets the tone with remarks like: 'So that is our son, Rachel . . . he is a Harford, every inch of him,' and 'Well, Rachel, what is over is over.' The switch to Christian names is arresting: it was all titles earlier, even over the tea table. Now we are in a more private, even domestic world with a man and woman talking about their past and quarrelling over their son. Mrs Arbuthnot does not indeed fall into his intimate style but the fact that she continues to address him as Lord Illingworth is clearly a deliberate expression of resentment. Only once there is a fleeting intimation of the affection she once felt and then she does abandon the formal style, pleading, 'George, don't take my son away from me.'

As the two recall the past, the audience's sympathies are delicately manipulated, divided as they would be in life. Mrs Arbuthnot has undeniably had the worst of it in the love affair but we can see that her bitterness makes her exaggerate, as when she spits at Illingworth's promise to do well for his son: 'Are you talking of the child you abandoned? Of the child who, as far as you were concerned, might have died of hunger and of want?' He reminds her, reasonably, it must seem, that it was she who left him and talk of leaving the child to starve is 'untrue and silly' because his mother had offered her six hundred a year. Of course what he passes over is the brutal fact that he refused to marry her, yet it is poignant as well as ironical that warmer feelings rise up in the cool dandy in the presence of the last person in the world to encourage them. His faint impulse to remorse ('I wasn't much older than you at the time'), his undisguised delight in his son, are simply taken as one more proof of his selfishness. This is indeed the fault each attributes to the other:

LORD ILLINGWORTH: My dear Rachel, I must candidly say that I think Gerald's future considerably more important than your past.

MRS ARBUTHNOT: Gerald cannot separate his future from my past.

LORD ILLINGWORTH: That is exactly what he should do. That is exactly what you should help him to do. What a typical woman you are! You talk sentimentally and you are thoroughly selfish the whole time.

The common sense point of view (as it may well seem) prevails, and Mrs Arbuthnot gives way to the pressure from Gerald and Illingworth, assenting reluctantly to her son's taking up the post, because she cannot explain to him why he should not.

In the third act Wilde tips the balance of sympathy rather more towards the woman. Once Illingworth is alone with his son, confident of having won his own way, he shows the *louche* side of his nature: Mrs Arbuthnot did after all have some reason for anxiety about Gerald's exposure to his influence. Contemporary reviewers tended to agree: 'the smoking room is the proper theatre for such displays.'[6] He is not just joking when he advises his son to cultivate the art of the trivial, learn how to tie his tie and conduct a dinner conversation: 'A man who can dominate a London dinner table can dominate the world. The future belongs to the dandy.' For along with this advice go sardonic comments on the 'good' women who 'have such limited views of life'. There is a sneer as well as sharp social criticism in the remark, also, perhaps, an attempt to break from the unusual emotionalism to which he has been subjected in the scene with Mrs Arbuthnot. It is understandable but a sign of moral coarseness. His jokes take on a mechanical quality which some critics have seen as a lapsing into self-indulgent wit on Wilde's part. In fact it is dramatically appropriate, an expression of the character's wish to display himself before his son, like a peacock:

LORD ILLINGWORTH: The history of women is the history of the worst form of tyranny the world has

112

ever known. The tyranny of the weak over the strong.
It is the only tyranny that lasts.
GERALD: But haven't women got a refining influence?
LORD ILLINGWORTH: Nothing refines but the intellect.

When the rest of the party return to the stage, Lady
Hunstanton as usual intensely curious to know what Lord
Illingworth has been talking about, Mrs Arbuthnot listens
tensely to what on the surface is simply a brittle exchange
of wit. Wilde's method is at its most intricate in this scene:
there is certainly a sub-text to be observed. When, for
instance, Lady Hunstanton enquires of Mrs Arbuthnot
'And how is your beautiful embroidery going on?', and
she replies 'I am always at work', the apparently
noncommittal remark hints at her bitter resentment at
having been obliged to devote her life to embroidery and
'good works'. (Another Hawthorne echo here: Hester
Prynne too had to use her skill in embroidery to support
herself and her fatherless child, as well as sew the letter 'A'
for her own shame.) A further ironical contrast is made
with the Archdeacon's image of his wife as a happy
Dorcas. The gout has crippled her fingers, though she was
very deft with her needle once: 'But she has many other
amusements. She is very much interested in her own
health.' It is like a caricature of Illingworth's complacency
and Mrs Arbuthnot's self-absorption; yet of course it is
also funny in itself, one of the many amusing moments
that keep the comic surface intact, although so much
restless thought and feeling is moving underneath it. The
scene runs down, the fireworks fade away, Lord
Illingworth goes onto the terrace with Mrs Allonby to look
at the 'inconstant' moon, followed eagerly by Gerald, and
Mrs Arbuthnot is left alone to assimilate all the conflicting
emotions the scene has roused.

Wilde makes it clear in the soliloquy which follows (she is agitated by the bad news that Gerald is to leave for India with Lord Illingworth) that her feeling for her son is desperately over-possessive. 'Let him leave me if he chooses,' she cries, 'but not with him – not with him! I couldn't bear it.' Then Hester appears, to make an appeal for Mrs Arbuthnot's friendship, and a dialogue loaded with irony develops, for in seeking endorsement from the woman she admires, Hester unconsciously rubs salt in a very sore wound:

> HESTER: A woman who has sinned should be punished, shouldn't she?
>
> MRS ARBUTHNOT: Yes. . . .
>
> HESTER: And the man should be punished in the same way?
>
> MRS ARBUTHNOT: In the same way. And the children, if there are children, in the same way also?
>
> HESTER: Yes, it is right that the sins of the parents should be visited on the children. It is a just law. It is God's law.
>
> MRS ARBUTHNOT: It is one of God's terrible laws.

Mrs Arbuthnot's acceptance of this grim puritan ethos has not improved her character, as we see when, alone with her son, she uses Hester's moral generalisations to nip the romance in the bud: 'I fear you need have no hopes of Miss Worsley. I know her views on life.' Gerald instinctively feels the unfairness: his mother's hints at Illingworth's bad character seem to him just part of her now irritating unworldliness. Finally, she is obliged to tell him her own story, though still she preserves her secret by telling it in the third person: 'Gerald, there was a girl once, she was very young, she was little over eighteen at the time . . .'.

114

There is an interesting distribution of sympathy at this point. As she tells the story we feel the seriousness it has for her, and it is poignant: 'George Harford' is so vividly there in her memory, with his solemn promise to marry the young girl, so 'ignorant of what life really is'.

But as her emotionalism increases we begin to resist, as Gerald does, and as some contemporary reviewers did. Even in 1893, when most people subscribed to the morality upheld by Hester and Mrs Arbuthnot, there were questions about why the latter need make quite so much fuss about her past. As William Archer put it, Mrs Arbuthnot is in easy circumstances, has a model son, seems not to suffer social slights, doesn't repent of her sin. 'Well, then, what is all this melodrama about?'[7] Exactly so. But wasn't this just the question Wilde wanted his audience to ask? Why had the agony of the 'woman with a past' ever been necessary, why need Frou-Frou have been cut off forever from her child, why, in the same year as Wilde's play, did Paula Tanqueray have to shoot herself? Why any of those miseries? Because society had ordained it.

By the radical change of context which placed the agonised woman in a more refined *intellectual* environment, Wilde made his audience see the traumatic situation as he had always seen it – as a quite unnecessary form of suffering.

Of course Mrs Arbuthnot cannot see it this way. She, poor woman, is trapped in her time, not free of it, as Wilde was. Wilde understands her psychology very well, better than William Archer, who confusedly felt that she should have the same view of things as her playwright, and fretfully deplored her lack of perspective, suggesting that it would be more telling 'if she took the situation more ironically and less tragically, if she answered the man of the world in the tone of a woman of the world'. But Mrs

Arbuthnot is not a Mrs Erlynne, let alone a Wilde. She does not question society's conventional judgments but takes up her role as martyred outcast with a passionate will to play it to the full. Archer noted that Mrs Bernard Beere, creating the role, 'looked magnificent in her black robe and Magdalen-red hair'. 'Magdalen-red hair' is exactly right for the impression Mrs Arbuthnot conveys of performing the penitent in a religious drama. It is her determination to play on the highest level, wearing the tragic mask, that makes her such an interesting character.

Interesting, not necessarily sympathetic. She is anything but sympathetic, really, when she overdoes the rhetoric, describing herself as 'a woman who drags a chain like a guilty thing', 'a woman who wears a mask, like a thing that is a leper', a 'lost soul'. Gerald's reaction is sensible, and insensitive: it all sounds very tragic, he says dismissively, but probably the girl was as much to blame as Lord Illingworth. The nemesis Illingworth prophesied has arrived. He warned her that she was bringing up her son in such a way that he would be a 'bitter judge' of her actions and so it is. With awful pomposity Gerald rules that no really nice girl would leave her home with a man to whom she was not married. It is more than his mother can bear: she is just withdrawing her objection to Gerald's joining Lord Illingworth when the action takes a sudden turn towards the melodrama which has up to now been fended off by the wit and the naturalism.

A full-scale melodramatic tableau is set up when Hester rushes into the room begging Gerald's protection from Illingworth who has 'horribly insulted' her, Gerald puts himself into an attitude of attack – 'As there is a God in heaven I will kill you!' – and Mrs Arbuthnot can only part the men by making her confession: 'Stop, Gerald, stop! He is your own father!' The early reviews commonly chose this scene for pictorial illustration of the play: Mrs Arbuthnot kneeling on the ground in shame, Gerald threatening his father. It is hard to know which of the actors has the most difficult task; Hester begging to be 'saved' when she has only been kissed, Gerald mouthing insults at Illingworth for insulting the 'purest thing on God's earth', or Mrs Arbuthnot obliged to utter so crude a curtain line.

After the finesse of the earlier dialogue the lurch into the high-pitched melodramatic style is certainly disconcerting. Archer mocked good-humouredly: 'It would be a just retribution if Mr Wilde were presently to be confronted with this tableau, in all the horrors of chromolithography, on every hoarding in London, with the legend, "Stay, Gerald! He is your father!" in crinkly letters in the corner'.[7]

Wilde might not have regarded it as retribution at all. 'I took that situation from *The Family Herald*', he is reported as saying. He was not ashamed of the links between his plays and the popular culture: Alan Bird maintains that they are a source of strength, even in this difficult act, and I think it is so, though very clever playing would be required to see us through the 'chromo-lithography' sequence. For there is psychological probability in the movement to melodrama at this point. The cause of the violence is trivial; it was only a kiss, but given the personalities concerned – the intense, humourless girl, the over-strained mother, the naïve young man – it is not surprising that it has precipitated them out of the world of civilised, controlled behaviour and subtle talk into the more primitive world of feeling.

There might be ways of performing this climax which would use the exaggerated physical attitudes to suggest the very real obsessions in which the characters are trapped. Mrs Arbuthnot's position on the ground 'in shame' before her own son catches with vivid physicality the normally hidden distortions of feeling in the peculiar relationship between mother and son. Through the tableau too we receive an impression of the inner turmoil in Gerald which he could never express in words. Does he see the image of the 'saintly' mother dissolving as he grasps her hands and looks into her face while she sinks to the ground? Her abject reaction suggests that she sees something in his expression that frightens her; we must wonder too how he can endure the shattering of his illusions and the emotional embarrassment of having to see his mother as a mistress, the kindly patron as her lover and his father. Will he turn on her? Are we heading for the ugly, violent climax which the oedipal implications of his relationship with his mother might well demand? Wilde holds a pause, to allow us these questionings. It is 'after a time' – a most deliberate stage direction – that Gerald resolves his turmoil, raises his mother up and, putting his arm round her, leads her from the room.

It is the play's turning point. With the breaking of the tableau goes the break-up of the stereotyped moral attitudes represented by the mother kneeling 'in shame' with the seducer standing by and the puritanical girl turning away. These outworn attitudes are to be replaced in the final act by remarkably radical views which refuse the postures of the old melodrama.

Appropriately for this new radicalism there is a bold change of setting. The revolution could not occur in Lady Hunstanton's mansion, the old system is too well established there. Instead, Lady Hunstanton and Mrs Allonby are made to come to Mrs Arbuthnot and survey her modest sitting room with its books and flowers ('Quite the happy English home,' Mrs Allonby sneers) and speculate on the effect the 'goodness' reflected here would

have on Lord Illingworth. Through it all runs the familiar
note of equivocation. Lady Hunstanton is impressed by
the contents of the room – 'books that don't shock one,
pictures that one can look at without blushing' – until Mrs
Allonby remarks coolly 'But I like blushing,' when she
blandly agrees: 'Well, there is a good deal to be said for
blushing, if one can do it at the proper moment.'

How would these two react if they knew the truth about
Mrs Arbuthnot and Lord Illingworth? Wilde never allows
that question to develop but gives strong hints towards an
answer. Everything we have seen of these worldly ladies
suggests that they would be quite likely to cover up and
pretend that nothing much had happened. It is one of the
most piercing ironies of a deeply ironical play that the
harsh judgment Mrs Arbuthnot has dreaded all her adult
life was passed on her by no one but herself. Words like
'sin' are not in the vocabulary of a Lady Hunstanton or a
Mrs Allonby.

Gerald, however, does not question the use of the word
'sin'; he is truly his mother's son in this respect (with a
layer of raw priggishness all his own). It is in a way
touching when, after the visitors' departure, he shows his
mother the letter he has written to Lord Illingworth
requiring him to marry her but his naïve amazement at her
refusal to be made an honest woman is comical: we are not
expected to take his peroration as earnestly as he does:

Mother, you make it terribly difficult for me by talking
like that; and I can't understand why you won't look at
this matter from the right, from the only proper
standpoint. It is to take away the bitterness out of your
life, to take away the shadow that lies on your name,
that this marriage must take place.

It was his mother who taught him this attitude by placing so much emphasis on the social aspect of her suffering; the fact that she was not married to her lover has been allowed to count for too much. It is true, of course, that society would regard her as disgraced and her seducer not: as she says, 'It is the usual history of a man and a woman as it usually happens, as it always happens. And the ending is the ordinary ending. The woman suffers. The man goes free.' We cannot blame Gerald, indeed must sympathise with him for refusing to accept this 'ordinary ending' for his mother. But he is insensitive in his inability to imagine why she should shrink from such a 'reparation'. Wilde cannot have failed to intend the bizarre comedy of their argument over whether his mother should marry his father:

GERALD: I implore you to do what I ask you.

MRS ARBUTHNOT: What son has ever asked of his mother to make so hideous a sacrifice? None.

GERALD: What mother has ever refused to marry the father of her own child? None.

Under the pressure of his obstinacy, the stereotyped social morality which she has allowed to damage her life finally loses its grip on her. She opposes to her son's conventional logic the full force of the passions which have been suppressed for so long. Out pours her bitter resentment of 'George Harford' (still she uses that name of the past) and of the 'saintly' life to which she was driven in her seclusion. She reveals too, more fully than perhaps she realises, how all her thwarted feelings and desire for 'the pleasant things of life' have come together in an intensity of love for her son which Wilde surely means us to see as unhealthy though understandable:

It is my dishonour that has made you so dear to me. It is my disgrace that has bound you so closely to me. It is the price I paid for you – the price of soul and body – that makes me love you as I do. Oh, don't ask me to do this horrible thing. Child of my shame, be still the child of my shame!

The last phrase was found difficult even by contemporary reviewers. Probably the only way to take it is as a kind of hysteria: the flood gates are opened, the concealment of twenty years is over; and she is talking to her son honestly for the first time in their lives. Even the unimaginative Gerald is shaken: 'Mother, I didn't know you loved me so much as that.' But he is obdurate: it is her 'duty' to marry his father. Then Hester comes to Mrs Arbuthnot's rescue. Illingworth is a man none of them now respects; how can a marriage with him make anything right? A woman's view emerges, distinctly different from the male view of things, more genuinely rational than Gerald's profit-and-loss book-keeping. Perhaps Mrs Arbuthnot is taking a small revenge when she reminds Hester of her so recent pharisaical attitude, but Hester's answer sets the tone which Wilde means to triumph:

MRS ARBUTHNOT: . . . . The sins of the parents should be visited on the children. It is God's law.
HESTER: I was wrong. God's law is only Love.

A happy ending of a kind is glimpsed: the three will settle in America, which Hester assures Mrs Arbuthnot is 'wiser and less unjust' than England. Gerald will no doubt be a mother's boy twice over, and the relationship of the trio will be rather too high-souled and sentimental for most tastes, but Mrs Arbuthnot may retrieve something from the ruins of her youthful life, some of the pleasure she so bitterly feels herself to have lost. And she has her son. This is supreme triumph over the man who would not marry her.

Wilde brings us finally to the *scène à faire* between the 'seducer' and his 'victim': the inadequacy of those *boulevard* terms to describe the relationship we have been shown is a measure of how radically he adapted the convention. Illingworth comes to patch things up and put the events of the night before into what seems to him (as perhaps to some of us) their true perspective: 'That silly Puritan girl making a scene merely because I wanted to kiss her. What harm is there in a kiss?' Her reply has the ring of a Mrs Alving's remorseless awareness of the past: 'A kiss may ruin a human life, George Harford. I know that. I know that too well.' As he goes on talking, ignoring her interruptions, mapping out *his* son's future, we are waiting for the moment when she will administer the *coup de grâce*. It has to come: his self-centred concentration on his own satisfaction makes us feel that, yet there is something appealing in the new warmth that has come into his character through his delight in his son. (He admires the boy all the more, he tells Mrs Arbuthnot, for leaping to Hester's defence as he did.)

When she directs him to the window to observe Gerald and Hester walking as lovers in the garden, telling him that they are all three going away together and he will never see them again, we may feel that there is some justice in his 'You have grown hard, Rachel.' 'I was very young at the time,' he says, 'We men know life too early.' But she gives him no quarter. To his 'Rachel, I want my son,' she returns a cold 'There is no room in my boy's life for *you*. He is not interested in you.' As she intently watches him reading the letter from Gerald, it seems that she is savouring in advance the sweet triumph which comes when he makes his patronising offer – 'To get my son back I am ready – yes, I am ready to marry you, Rachel' – and she refuses him. If, as Hester suggested, all women were martyred in Mrs Arbuthnot, now they are all revenged. Wilde's grasp of her psychology is impressive. He has sympathy for her as a symbol of womanhood and a suffering individual. Yet he shows that her love for her son has unpleasant aspects: it is inseparable from the hatred she feels for his father. 'They feed each other,' she says of these twin passions, with a self-knowledge which is chilling and makes it seem doubtful whether a happy ending is really possible for her.

The play has moved far from melodrama into analysis of Ibsen-like subtlety when the two of them face the situation their past actions have created:

LORD ILLINGWORTH: What sort of love is that which needs to have hate as its brother?

MRS ARBUTHNOT: It is the sort of love I have for Gerald. Do you think that terrible? Well, it is terrible. All love is terrible. All love is a tragedy. I loved you once, Lord Illingworth. Oh, what a tragedy for a woman to have loved you!

'And does my son hate me as you do?' he asks. 'He merely despises you,' she says. There is nothing to match the unsparing naturalism of this on the English stage of Wilde's time. We have to go to Ibsen for anything comparable. It is another Ibsen-like moment when Illingworth prepares to leave and the ghosts of their youthful past rise up in a strange moment of involuntary recall: 'How curious! At this moment you look exactly as you looked the night you left me twenty years ago. You have just the same expression in your mouth.' What is her expression? There is no record of how Mrs Bernard Beere conveyed that look, but perhaps it was tremulous in a youthful way, bringing up a memory of the real love they once had and the misery he, as well as she, may have experienced when she left him. From the ambiguous moment, with its potential poignancy, Wilde audaciously switches to sudden brutality as Illingworth pulls himself out of the past back to the humiliating reality of rejection and characteristically restores his self-respect with an insult: 'It's been an amusing experience to have met amongst people of one's own rank, and treated quite seriously too, one's mistress and one's –.'

She cuts off the unforgivable word with violence, striking him in the face with his own glove, the abortive act of *Lady Windermere's Fan*. Contemporary reviewers were much put out by this scene, finding it hard to believe that the 'polished profligate' who had up to then at least been a gentleman, would suddenly turn into a 'tap-room blackguard'. It was just this touching faith in the image of the 'gentleman' that Wilde was assailing. The episode allows a curtain line in which the revenge of women is given its most triumphant expression. Gerald picks up the dropped glove and asks what visitor has called, giving Mrs Arbuthnot the cue for the devastating last line: 'Oh! no one. No one in particular. A man of no importance.'

It is not too surprising that *A Woman of No Importance*, though attracting attention and audiences as all Wilde's plays did by then, did not enjoy quite the popularity of its predecessor. The message is bitter, the re-writing of the theatrical convention and the messages it carries radical and uncompromising. The reviewer for the *Illustrated London News*, though conceding that Wilde's thesis 'on behalf of the "woman's revolt" ' was perfectly defensible, suspected that 'many playgoers at the Haymarket resented the contemptuous dismissal of the man, his cheek tingling with the sounding buffet administered by the lady.' Though he makes an ironic comment on that response – 'the resources of womanly forgiveness are conventionally supposed to be inexhaustible' – he evidently shared it to some extent for he concludes his account of Mrs Bernard Beere's praiseworthy attempt at the difficult character of Mrs Arbuthnot with the disapproving comment: 'It is not her fault that she has to strike Mr Tree in the face with his own glove, a climax which is a great injustice to both.'

The play is an experiment in style which makes taxing demands on actors and director – and critics. But it is undoubtedly one of Wilde's most original and interesting achievements, as we can appreciate more easily if we approach it along lines running to Chekhov, Henry James, English melodrama, rather than always to Sheridan, comedy of manners and so forth. The beauty and the difficulty of the play lies just in this, that Wilde will not be bound by the old categories but allows his wit to play on what could be tragic and his seriousness to creep in through the epigrams.

7
'An Ideal Husband'

*First performed 3 January 1895, Haymarket Theatre,
London.*
Published 1895.

There could not be such a thing as an 'ideal husband', Mrs
Allonby had decided. In his new play, again performed at
the Haymarket, with a new actor-manager, Lewis Waller,
as Lord Chiltern, Wilde takes a closer look at this
proposition and at the situation of the man called on to fill
that uncomfortable role. It is a 'man with a past' this time;
the Puritan woman (for she is here again) is his wife, which
adds to the agony and at times brings the comedy close to
tragedy.

There is a 'woman with a past' in *An Ideal Husband* but
she is a far cry from the suffering women of earlier plays: a
hard-boiled adventuress, this one, for whom the term
'woman with a past' has no terrors. Wilde seems to have
decided that it was time for it to cease to terrify anyone.
The type had acquired rather too much pseudo-tragic

glamour through Mrs Patrick Campbell's rendering of the conventionally 'guilty' Paula in *The Second Mrs Tanqueray* in 1893. Wilde cuts it down to size in *An Ideal Husband*. When Sir Robert Chiltern, writhing in the toils of the adventuress, asks Lord Goring whether he might not be able to use her past against her – 'She looks like a woman with a past, doesn't she?' – he receives a reply which puts the whole thing in proportion:

> Most pretty women do. But there is a fashion in pasts just as there is a fashion in frocks. Perhaps Mrs Cheveley's past is merely a slight décolleté one, and they are excessively popular nowadays.

Of all Wilde's comedies this has the most wide-ranging implications as a criticism of English society. We are at the heart of power in the Chilterns' house: these lords and ladies really do rule England. Chiltern is a minister so influential that if he speaks in the House of Commons in favour of a highly dubious Argentine Canal scheme the chances are that it will be accepted. Everyone seems to be or to have a relative in the Government. Lady Markby, for instance, deplores the effect of politics on her husband's temper and plants the insidious idea that the House of Commons, in trying to become useful, 'does a great deal of harm'. Always in the background is the reality of the wider world of politics and government, seen from within the parish of Westminster as well as St James's and also from a European angle. Mrs Cheveley comes into the scene from Vienna where 'our attachés are very interested in her'; she continually refers to European standards, to the disadvantage of the English, and though the tone of her sneers damns her rather than the targets of her cynicism, she manages to raise disturbing questions about the extent of the corruption in this society.

Private life is very firmly related to public life. Sir Robert tries hard to resist the connection: '. . . public and private life are different things. They have different laws, and move on different lines.' But his wife is adamant: 'They should both represent man at his highest.'

Whether or not 'man at his highest', it is certainly man at his most powerful and wealthy that is shown in the sumptuous stage image which opens the play. In the octagon room at the Chilterns' house in Grosvenor Square Lady Chiltern stands at the head of a staircase, receiving her guests as they ritualistically ascend. They are the Establishment. The Earl of Caversham wears the riband and star of the Garter and is a 'good' specimen of the aristocracy. (Lady Markby draws attention to the other kind in her candid comments on the 'weak' brain of the Duke of Maryborough: 'His good father was just the same. There is nothing like race, is there?') The scene makes a large statement about style, a major preoccupation of this play: Lady Chiltern is like a goddess receiving initiates, with all around a display of beautiful and splendid possessions; the great chandelier with wax lights over the well of the staircase and the icon it illuminates, a large eighteenth-century French tapestry 'representing the Triumph of Love, from a design by Boucher'. Wilde means this tapestry to be a dominating scenic image.

Everything in this first scene, including the characters, is described in terms of works of art. Lady Chiltern is a woman of 'grave Greek beauty'; the two ladies who open the dialogue with languid gossip, sitting on a *Louis Seize* sofa, are 'types of exquisite fragility' whom, we are told, Watteau would have loved to paint. Lord Caversham, in his Garter insignia, is 'rather like a portrait by Lawrence' while Mabel Chiltern is 'like a Tanagra statuette'. Visual taste leans to the eighteenth century (a suggestion here of nostalgia on Wilde's part for Augustan civility and rationalism). In strong contrast is the more exotic effect created by Mrs Cheveley. She is 'like an orchid' with Venetian red hair and a thin mouth like a line of scarlet. Lord Goring in the next scene says of her appearance at the party the night before that she wore far too much rouge and not quite enough clothes ('Tawny-haired, red-cheeked, white-shouldered,' said Archer of the first Mrs Cheveley').[1] All signs, these, of something not quite right: she is 'a work of art on the whole, but showing the influence of too many schools'. This aesthetically dubious style accurately expresses her dubious morals. Similarly Sir Robert Chiltern's style expresses his complex, divided personality. Wilde sees him as a Vandyke and spends a great deal of time in the stage directions explaining how the striking contrast between his mouth and eyes should guide us in our interpretation of his character: 'an almost complete separation of passion and intellect, as though thought and emotion were each isolated in its own sphere through some violence of will-power'. The most perfect stylist of the play, Lord Goring, is not given a painter to himself, perhaps because he is, as Mabel Chiltern demurely suggests, 'in a category of his own'. He is, says Wilde, a 'flawless dandy' with a well-bred expressionless face who plays with life and 'is on perfectly good terms with the world'.

Wilde's handling of the dialogue in the intricate party scene is a triumph of orchestration. Different tunes are heard as the characters move about the stage, group and regroup, in search of partners, gossip, supper. We recognise a general 'key' or house style from which no one departs too far: it is formal, balanced, rich in ironical nuances and double entendres. Leit motifs float into the air from the 'choral' sections, as when Lady Basildon and Mrs Marchmont discuss husbands ('My Reginald is quite hopelessly faultless'), and distinct instrumental groups emerge; the chilly duet of Lady Chiltern and Mrs Cheveley, the buoyant trio of Lord Goring, his father (the Earl of Caversham) and Mabel Chiltern. The vocal tones of the last three are sharply contrasted – Lord Caversham gruff and bluff in aristocratic no-nonsense style; his son the epitome of amused languor; Mabel Chiltern archly provocative. They challenge one another but create effects of harmony, not dissonance. The Earl may growl at his son, but when he accuses him, as he does at regular intervals, of being 'heartless' we know he is waiting for the reply which is always given (and we guess is genuinely meant): 'I hope not, father.' Throughout the play the little movements of kindness and humour among these 'trivial' people form a vital counterpoint to the agonies of the 'earnest' ones.

Brilliantly, through this frivolous overture, Wilde conveys a sense of the close relation between political power and social acceptability and gives hints, as in Mrs Cheveley's mocking reference to 'family skeletons', that a gulf is about to open up between the impeccable appearances and the hidden life of the characters. Her function is to activate a drama of retribution and conscience which bears obvious marks of Wilde's indebtedness to the *boulevard* playwrights (Scribe, Sardou's *Dora*) and – more importantly – of his interest in Ibsen.[2] *Hedda Gabler* was still working in his imagination, to judge from the scenes between Mrs Cheveley and Lady Chiltern (like Hedda and Thea Elvsted, they were antagonists as schoolgirls). So too *Pillars of Society*. That first play of Ibsen's seen in London (at the Gaiety Theatre in 1880) was performed in 1889 with Elizabeth Robins, whose Hedda was so much admired by Wilde, as Martha Bernick: Shaw commented on her 'beautiful Puritan charm' in the part. *Pillars of Society* offered a good model for a playwright with Wilde's preoccupations. Its central character, the 'pillar of society', is threatened with the uncovering of a disreputable episode from his past on which his fortunes have been based and is finally brought – by the impact of his corrupt actions on his own family – to confession and regeneration (of a kind). These are Scribean themes too, but *Pillars of Society* showed how they could be given more subtle treatment. In this sense, Wilde is closer to Ibsen than to the French predecessors on whom they both drew.

Boulevard characteristics are most marked in Wilde's treatment of Mrs Cheveley. Shaw liked her because she was a 'real' adventuress – 'selfish, dishonest and third rate' – not a sentimentalised stage one. She has to be like this, we can see, to put the requisite pressure on Sir Robert: she presents him too with a dark mirror image of the self he has refused to recognise. Wilde's skill in alienation techniques is never better shown than in the scenes involving these two. The audience is free to concentrate on issues since neither character attracts much sympathy: Mrs Cheveley is a brutal cynic, Sir Robert an uneasy actor. In his initial meeting with Mrs Cheveley, he plays the dandy, a role which does not suit him, and when she opens the subject of the Argentine Canal Company by reminding him of his own involvement in the Suez Canal scheme (Wilde was again looking out to history at this point), he plays the perfect hypocrite:

> Yes. But the Suez Canal was a very great and splendid undertaking. It gave us our direct route to India. It had imperial value. It was necessary that we should have

control. This Argentine scheme is a commonplace Stock Exchange swindle.

'A speculation, Sir Robert,' she says, 'A brilliant, daring speculation,' whereupon he takes up a still holier-than-thou stance:

Believe me, Mrs Cheveley, it is a swindle. Let us call things by their proper names. It makes matters simpler.

Earlier she had dropped a sinister name from the past: 'I hear your pictures are charming. Poor Baron Arnheim – you remember the Baron? – used to tell me you had some wonderful Corots.' Now Chiltern tries to turn her to the acceptable side of the mysterious interests which link him with the dead Baron, inviting her to accompany him to the music-room to see the celebrated pictures: 'Corots seem to go with music, don't they?' Mrs Cheveley, however, is not to be diverted by what she contemptuously calls 'silver twilights or rose-pink dawns'. 'Politics are my only pleasure,' she had said in their first guarded conversation. She is at the party because it is here that the politics of England are decided, as Sir Robert makes clear:

. . . The success of the Canal depends, of course, on the attitude of England, and I am going to lay the report of the Commissioners before the House tomorrow night.

Corots in the music-room; the world waiting to hear Chiltern's statement: he is allowed to climb to the height of his power before Mrs Cheveley sets in motion the process of bringing him down. It is classical hubris (Wilde points this up with his emphasis on the classical restriction of time to twenty-four hours).

Mrs Cheveley drops her bombshell – 'Withdraw the report that you had intended to lay before the House' – with casual brutality (and contemptuous familiarity with the way politicians renege). Sadistically, she keeps her hand concealed to the last moment, evidently enjoying his indignant show of moral superiority – 'You have lived so long abroad, Mrs Cheveley, that you seem to be unable to realise that you are talking to an English gentleman' – before deflating him: 'I realise that I am talking to a man who laid the foundation of his fortune by selling to a Stock Exchange speculator a Cabinet secret.' In a diabolically neat reversal she quotes his own words against him: 'It was a swindle, Sir Robert. Let us call things by their proper names. It makes everything simpler.'

It is the first time on Wilde's stage that a powerful Establishment male figure has been confronted by so formidable and ruthless an adversary. Wilde cannot have liked her (any more than we do) but he must surely have found satisfaction in letting her loose on the hypocritical self-righteousness of the 'pillars of society'. Only someone as hard as she is could penetrate the carapace of complacency which prevents Sir Robert from seeing the ironic likeness she points out between his action of the past and hers now. 'It is infamous,' he gasps when she lays out her blackmailing proposal: if he will withdraw his opposition to the Argentine scheme, she will give him back the self-incriminating letter he wrote to Arnheim. It gives the blackmailer cold pleasure to draw the moral and bring out the neatness of the nemesis: 'You made your own fortune out of one canal. You must help me and my friends to make our fortunes out of another.' She warns him what his fate will be if she hands the letter to a newspaper:

Nowadays, with our modern mania for morality,

everyone has to pose as a paragon of purity, incorruptibility, and all the other seven deadly virtues – and what is the result? You all go over like ninepins one after the other . . . . And yours is a very nasty scandal. You couldn't survive it.

Wilde comes very close to his own delicate situation in this prophetic statement: in only a few months the scandal of his homosexuality was to convulse the society whose portrait he draws in the play. Perhaps his awareness of what might be in store, though repressed, has made its way in and invested with remarkable intensity the lines in which Mrs Cheveley envisages the 'loathsome joy' of the newspaper scandalmongers. 'Think of the hypocrite with his greasy smile penning his leading article and arranging the foulness of the public placard.' It is a horrific vision: one cannot be surprised that Sir Robert succumbs and accepts her conditions. Mrs Cheveley is given her head in this scene in order to make a general attack on the hypocrisy of society, as well as instigate processes of psychological change in the central characters. We are not invited to empathise with her, but her cynical views cannot be dismissed for they are often right. She is certainly right to warn him (a warning Wilde might have taken to himself): 'You have a splendid position, but it is your splendid position that makes you so vulnerable.'

There are limits on her understanding, however. When she tells Chiltern that she understood his nature from the first ('I analysed you, though you did not adore me'), she is over-confident, for she has not totally understood him: as Goring later points out, Chiltern's 'real self' is not to be equated with his lower self. Her cynicism has distortions which are in the end to prove more crippling than the mistakes made by the other characters.

When Chiltern and his wife are alone together at the close of the act, Wilde offers yet another variation on the puritan temperament. Lady Chiltern's weakness, he explained to a journalist, is the feminine passion 'for making ideals'; her husband's the masculine weakness of not daring 'to show his imperfections to the thing he loves'.[3] The actress who created the role, Julia Neilson, hated the character ('An impossible prig') and found it hard to play her. It is another instance of the demands Wilde makes on his actors: Lady Chiltern must both attract and repel sympathy. She is priggish and naïve in her worship of her husband's moral greatness – 'You have never let the world soil you' – and certainly inexorable in her insistence that he 'be that ideal still'. We begin to feel more sympathy for Sir Robert; it is a hard fate to be ground between two millstones such as his wife and Mrs Cheveley.

Yet we can also see that so merciless a sifting is needed. As he struggles to evade her stern questioning, he shows in full the dishonesty which is an unhappy link between him and Mrs Cheveley (even at school, says his wife, the adventuress had been 'untruthful, dishonest, an evil influence . . . she stole things, she was a thief'). The hypocritical evasions become desperate but always he comes up against the unbending Puritan morality: 'It can never be necessary to do what is not honourable.' When for the second time he submits to the orders of a woman, sitting down to write at his wife's dictation that he will not support the dishonest scheme, he has gained a very uneasy respite. 'Love me always,' he begs her and back comes the chilling reply, 'I will love you always, because you will always be worthy of love.'

There is more threat than reassurance in this, as Sir Robert evidently recognises. Alone on the stage he calls to

the servant 'Put out the lights, Mason, put out the lights.'
As the servant is already doing just that, the line is clearly
meant less as a practical direction than as a conscious
quotation, bearing the ominous suggestion that this
marriage, like Othello's, may be dragged down and
destroyed by lies. In the near darkness into which the stage
has been plunged one source of light remains, the great
chandelier, illuminating the tapestry of the Triumph of
Love. Is this a symbol of hope or of irony? Impossible to
say, any more than to know whether Lady Chiltern will
prove right in her belief that people are the prisoners of
their past and cannot change.

By the rise of the curtain for the second act a great step
has been taken; Sir Robert has succeeded in making his
confession, not to his wife but to Lord Goring, lounging in
the Chilterns' morning room, in usual debonair style. The
confessional structure of this act takes Wilde very close to
Ibsen; one admission leads to another till we have
penetrated further into the closely guarded interior life
than would have seemed possible in the glossy opening
sequences. As he expands in the relief of confessing to a
sympathetic auditor, we begin to see how deeply Sir Robert
is corrupted, and are given a strange new light on the art
treasures in his house. Tapestries, enamels, jewels, carved
ivory were what Arnheim dangled before the young,
ambitious man as symbols of luxury, before going on to
assert that such things were no more than 'a painted scene
in a play', a background to the one thing worth having –
'power, power over other men, power over the world'.
Chiltern swallowed the whole doctrine, including
Arnheim's idea that only the rich could achieve this power:
wealth therefore had to be his objective.

'A thoroughly shallow creed', says Goring, speaking
'with great deliberation' and a moral seriousness which

draws from his friend only a remarkably unregenerate self-
defence: 'Wealth has given me enormous power. It gave
me at the very outset of my life freedom, and freedom is
everything. You have never been poor, and never known
what ambition is.' Shaw thought Chiltern's 'assertion of
the individuality and courage of his wrongdoing as against
the mechanical idealism of his stupidly good wife' struck
the 'modern note'; 'the philosophy in which the scene was
based,' he said, produced 'the most pregnant epigrams in
the play, and was the only philosophy that ever has
produced epigrams'.[4] He is exaggerating somewhat; Wilde
obviously has a sympathetic interest in Chiltern's
individualism, but he gives Goring the best epigrams, as
well as many telling low-key responses which do eventually
sober his friend and make him think again. Goring's
jesting is seen not to be random but to reflect a coherent
philosophy. When Chiltern tells his friend how he has
superstitiously tried to 'disarm destiny' by distributing to
public charities sums far in excess of what he received from
Arnheim, Goring's riposte, which might earlier have
seemed merely flippant, strikes deep ('Dear me! what a lot
of harm you must have done'), as does his analysis of
Chiltern's political dilemma:

> However, in your case, Robert, a confession would not
> do. The money, if you will allow me to say so, is . . .
> awkward. Besides, if you did make a clean breast of the
> whole affair, you would never be able to talk morality
> again. And in England a man who can't talk morality
> twice a week to a large, popular, immoral audience is
> quite over as a serious politician.

The confessional sequence becomes increasingly emotional
as Chiltern lets his imagination face his true situation and

137

the public disgrace that is in store for him: 'It is as if a hand of ice were laid upon one's heart.' At the same time Wilde is looking rather cursorily after the mechanics of a plot which is not, despite all appearances, leading to tragedy. Lord Goring reveals his own past relationship with Mrs Cheveley, a hint to be added to the mystery over the diamond brooch lost by one of the guests (Wilde spoke of *An Ideal Husband* as his 'mystery' play and obviously enjoyed this aspect of it, perhaps more than we do).

Lady Chiltern is then given a chance to show a more appealing side of her personality. She comes in looking less regal, in walking dress, back from a meeting of the Woman's Liberal Association where, she smilingly tells Lord Goring, when he teases her about women's bonnets, she has been engaged on 'dull, useful, delightful things, Factory Acts, Female Inspectors, the Eight Hours Bill, the Parliamentary Franchise'. She is a thoroughly Shavian woman at this point, close cousin to Vivie Warren, with her preference for actuarial conveyancing over conventional 'feminine' pleasures. In 1893 Wilde had complimented Shaw on *Widowers' Houses* ('Op.2 of the great Celtic School'):[5] 'I like your superb confidence in the dramatic value of the mere facts of life. I admire the horrible flesh and blood of your creatures . . . ' *An Ideal Husband* is the 'op. 5' he was 'itching' to get at when he wrote to Shaw: it has more Shavian realism than any other of his plays.

Like everyone else, Lady Chiltern responds to Lord Goring's charm, but her mind remains closed: when he drops the dandy and hints at the need for tolerance, since all are imperfect, she fends him off with a blue stocking joke – 'Are you a Pessimist? What will the other dandies say? They will all have to go into mourning' – an oblique reference to Schopenhaurian ideas, to which Goring responds with a full-throated statement of his counter-philosophy: 'Life cannot be understood without much charity . . . It is love, and not German philosophy, that is the true explanation of this world . . .'.

Lady Chiltern cannot really understand what he means by charity. Her failure casts a dark shadow over the whole idea of marriage, already under attack from the cynical Mrs Cheveley (she has had two bad marriages). Wilde provides more hopeful evidence in the charming flirtation of Goring and Mabel Chiltern which slips in gaily whenever opportunity offers and always changes the key, as Mabel does at the close of the emotional scene with Lady Chiltern, entering 'in the most ravishing frock' and telling Goring, 'Pray be as trivial as you can'. Mabel makes no claim to have a philosophy of life, but her clear-eyed view of things encourages optimism about the marriage to which she and Lord Goring are so evidently moving (though never fast enough for Lord Caversham). No ideal husbands for her; when reminded that one of her suitors has a brilliant future, she jokes: 'Oh! I wouldn't marry a man with a future before him for anything under the sun.' Wilde wants there to be no doubt that despite her frivolity she is on the side of the angels. He fits her, rather portentously perhaps, into the symbolic scheme of the Boucher tapestry, the Triumph of Love. She is taking part in a tableau which she amusingly describes as the 'Triumph of something, I don't know what!' (Her part is to stand on her head.) The connection with the Boucher could easily be missed by audiences (who seldom see Wilde's design carried out clearly enough to point the symbolism) but the arcane little reference shows us how seriously Wilde wants us to take Mabel and her love affair. She is a figure of life, and he thoroughly approves her unashamed pursuit of Lord Goring: ('I hope it will be the triumph of me. Only triumph I am really interested in at present.') In her exuberant warmth of character she is a far cry both from her 'perfect' sister-in-law and the detested Mrs Cheveley. To the latter she is almost rude, giving only 'a little nod' when Lady Chiltern introduces her to the 'dreadful woman'.

The unexpected visit of Lady Markby and Mrs Cheveley (the latter come in search of 'her' diamond brooch) provides the last choral comedy of the play. Lady Markby once again draws attention to obscure connections between public and private behaviour, with droll comments on the less than ideal performance of her husband: 'He has sadly degenerated. Really, this horrid House of Commons quite ruins our husbands for us.' Meanwhile Mrs Cheveley allows herself innuendoes she knows her senior will not be able to interpret, as when Lady Markby refers disparagingly to 'Blue Books' and she observes languidly: 'I have never read a Blue Book. I prefer books . . . in yellow covers.' In such a joke, as in her risqué comment on the curate ('I am afraid I am not fond of girl friends') she goes far beyond the freedoms taken by the worldly women of earlier plays. There seems an unbridgeable gulf between her and the intensely fastidious Lady Chiltern.

Yet the two women are brought close by profound dislike which gives them an intimate understanding of each other's motives and feelings. Their violent antagonism, belonging to the past and yet still so fresh, brings up in troubling form the insistent question of the play, 'Can people change?':

> MRS CHEVELEY: I see that after all these years you have not changed a bit, Gertrude.
> LADY CHILTERN: I never change.

MRS CHEVELEY (*elevating her eyebrows*): Then life has taught you nothing?

LADY CHILTERN: It has taught me that a person who has once been guilty of dishonest and dishonourable action may be guilty of it a second time and should be shunned.

MRS CHEVELEY: Would you apply that rule to everyone?

LADY CHILTERN: Yes, to everyone without exception.

MRS CHEVELEY: Then I am sorry for you, Gertrude, very sorry for you.

Perhaps she is, but it does not prevent her from applying the *coup de grâce* and bringing the house of illusion crashing down with her smooth response to Lady Chiltern's glacial snub – ('What has my husband to do with you? With a woman like you?') – 'Between you and him there are chasms. He and I are closer than friends. We are enemies linked together. The same sin binds us.' Sir Robert enters at this point; it is the timing of melodrama but the irony of Ibsen, as he stands there, hearing his wife order Mrs Cheveley to leave the house and receive the mocking reply: 'Your house! A house bought with the price of dishonour. A house, everything in which has been paid for by fraud.' Julia Neilson was not able to hold the stage in these strong scenes, according to Shaw: she was only satisfying as Lady Chiltern when she sat still, letting her beauty and grace be 'eloquent' for her. Mrs Cheveley evidently dominated, as she often does: the 'common' style proves the more robust, though it should not.

When husband and wife are alone, Wilde allows her a pathetic humanity. She, the fanatic for truth, begs him: 'Lie to me! Lie to me! Tell me it is not true!' Her collapse is pitiable but the sympathy is with Chiltern when he inveighs against her immature view of life: 'Why can't you women love us faults and all? Why do you place us on monstrous pedestals?' In the nakedness of his despair he even becomes for a time the mouthpiece of Wilde's philosophy of love and tolerance: 'All sins, except a sin against itself, Love should forgive.'

But he is still a long way from regeneration. Wilde is at his most realistic (and more probing than Shaw's analysis would suggest) when he shows how quickly the genuine agony leads into self-pity, then self-justification, till in the end he is accusing his wife of being responsible for the 'public disgrace, ruin, terrible shame' which lies before him if Mrs Cheveley carries out her threat to publicise his letter should he not make his speech in her favour in the House. All would have been well, he says, with almost unbelievable complacency, if his wife had not intervened: the sin of his youth that had risen up – 'with its hands at my throat' – could have been killed for ever, 'sent back into its tomb'. When the curtain comes down on this bleak ending it is hard to imagine how Wilde can find a way to a happy resolution.

In the third act he sets about the difficult task, transferring the scene from the Chiltern establishment to Lord Goring's bachelor rooms, where the 'faultless dandy' is glimpsed for a moment in another dimension, discussing buttonholes with the 'Ideal Butler', as if the horrors of 'earnestness' did not exist:

LORD GORING: ... For the future a more trivial buttonhole, Phipps, on Thursday evenings.

PHIPPS: I will speak to the florist my Lord. She has had a loss in her family lately, which perhaps accounts for the lack of triviality your lordship complains of in the buttonhole.

LORD GORING: Extraordinary thing about the lower

class in England – they are always losing their relations.

PHIPPS: Yes, my lord! They are extremely fortunate in that respect.

Lord Goring however cannot be allowed to move too far in the direction of *The Importance of Being Earnest*. He has to function in the more uncomfortable reality of a play which now turns highly melodramatic; the emotions dictate it, but also, it is clear, a happy ending cannot be achieved outside the convention.

Lady Chiltern's letter, on pink notepaper, with its ambiguous message, 'I want you. I trust you. I am coming to you,' is certainly rather crudely contrived to make an innocent plea for help sound like a love letter; Scribe does not seem far off here. But there are lights and shades in Wilde's melodrama. Lord Goring keeps his own style through it all, as in the conversations with his father who calls unexpectedly and to whom he gives his usual affectionate though exasperated attention ('Oh, why will parents always appear at the wrong time?').

The little scenes between father and son are a humanising element, though they also launch the melodrama plot; it is because he is pinned down by the Earl that Lord Goring has to leave it to Phipps to show the 'lady' into the drawing room, hence does not know that it is Mrs Cheveley, not Lady Chiltern, who calls. Lord Goring has to work almost as hard as a character in a French farce in this act, ushering unlooked for callers into the right rooms to keep them apart from each other, and having to conduct an intimate conversation with the least wanted visitor, Sir Robert, while believing that his wife is within inches of discovery in the drawing-room.

But though near to farce, as melodrama so often is (Eric

Bentley points out that standard definitions of farce would apply neatly to *Othello*), the scene allows for some psychological subtlety. It is an opportunity for Sir Robert to regain sympathy: his emotional account to his friend of the scene with his wife shows that his seeming complacency was only skin deep, that he is in fact deeply oppressed by a sense of his own unworthiness in relation to his wife: 'She does not know what weakness or temptation is . . . . She stands apart as good women do – pitiless in her perfection . . . cold and stern and without mercy.' Their childlessness makes an extra layer of hopelessness: 'Perhaps if God had sent us children she might have been kinder to me. But God has given us a lonely house.'

Wilde prepares the way out of this total bleakness with a garish *boulevard* turn. A chair carelessly overturned in the next room (Shaw found this the one unbelievable episode in the plot) alarms Sir Robert, who rushes in, to find Mrs Cheveley there; Lord Goring, remaining outside, goes on assuming that it is Lady Chiltern who has been discovered and whom he must therefore defend from her husband's inevitable suspicions. She is 'stainless and guiltless of all offence towards you', he declares, a baffling remark indeed in relation to Mrs Cheveley. Wilde handles the rather absurd mix-up with dash and confidence; probably he enjoyed the absurdity of the crossed-lines rhetoric in which the two men indulge. He certainly seems to enjoy the sequence where the full machinery of melodrama comes into play, as Mrs Cheveley turns her blackmailing on Lord Goring, offering him Chiltern's letter in return for Goring's promise to marry her. Some critics have found Wilde's treatment perfunctory at this point but it is quite probable that Mrs Cheveley would, as she says, be tired of living abroad and fancy a salon in London; also that on meeting Lord Goring again she should feel a revival of the old attraction: 'I knew you were the only person I had ever cared for, if I have ever cared for anybody, Arthur.' That last comment shows acuteness of self-analysis and is convincing in a way that Goring's supposed attachment to her in the past fails to be. He certainly has no feeling for her now: he uses his knowledge about the diamond brooch rather brutally to trap her, clasping it on her arm as a bracelet (she did not know it could be this), and threatening to call the police and charge her with theft (she stole the brooch from his cousin) unless she hands over the letter.

Everything has been brought down to the level of petty theft. It is not just a piece of crude melodramatic contrivance, for a sardonic connection between the small-scale dishonesty represented by the brooch and the large-scale dishonesty represented by the letter is boldly demonstrated by the stage image of the woman struggling in panic to release herself from the incriminating evidence and finally handing over that other piece of incriminating evidence which, as Lord Goring has deduced, she keeps in the bosom of her dress. 'For so well dressed a woman, Mrs Cheveley, you have moments of admirable common sense,' he says, as he burns the letter. It is one of his harder jokes, like his mocking repetition of her own words when she calls him a brute and coward: 'Oh! don't use big words. They mean so little.' He shows in this scene (as perhaps is needed) that he is no angel; maybe the 'faults' which Mabel Chiltern likes him for include a capacity for hardness, as well as the vanity which has him looking in mirrors and knocking years off his age.

By the end of the act Mrs Cheveley has moved out of the range of sympathy to become a figure of concentrated venom, her last act being yet another theft: she takes the other incriminating letter, Gertrude Chiltern's 'dying speech and confession' as she satirically calls it, telling Goring that she intends to send it to Sir Robert: 'I can't bear so upright a gentleman, so honourable an English gentleman, being so shamefully deceived . . . .' She goes from the play: there is no room for her in the last act which opens buoyantly with the love affair of Lord Goring and Mabel Chiltern speeding on its way to a happy conclusion. Shaw accused Wilde of being sentimental; perhaps he is elsewhere in the play, but he skilfully avoids excessive feeling in these scenes. The long deferred proposal of marriage is received with unsentimental pleasure:

> MABEL CHILTERN (*rapturously*): Oh, is it a proposal?
> LORD GORING (*somewhat taken aback*): Well, yes, it is –
>   I am bound to say it is.
> MABEL CHILTERN (*with a sigh of pleasure*): I am so glad.
>   That makes the second today.

The female dandy reduces the male dandy who never wants to be thought serious, to begging 'Mabel, do be serious. Please be serious,' not taking pity till he tells her in plain terms that he loves her and asks if she can love him a little in return. Then she admits to adoring him and he admits to his human vanity: he is a little over thirty he tells her 'after some hesitation', but she knows all about this; she takes him, as she indicated at the beginning, faults and all.

From the marriage that is so promising because rooted in realism we turn to the marriage that is threatened with disaster. Lord Goring tells Lady Chiltern that her husband is free of danger but that she has placed herself in an equivocal position because of her foolishly worded letter. Critics who see the letter and its aftermath as inflated and unconvincing cause for anxiety on her part rather miss the point. It is a criticism of her (surely intended by Wilde) that she is so terrified by the wrong construction that could be put on the letter and has so little faith in her husband's ability to react intelligently rather than with the mechanical 'idealism' which is her special fault. Wilde repeats an earlier stroke of irony by having her plead with Lord Goring to keep her secret, when he sensibly suggests that they tell Sir Robert the whole story. Puritan virtue is seen to be unreliable when it comes to telling the truth about one's own little errors.

The plot becomes excessively complicated to allow a way out of this impasse. Sir Robert returns from the House, having delivered a high-minded speech against the dubious Argentine scheme, to ecstatic applause ('one of the finest pieces of oratory ever delivered in the House since Canning'). He has received the letter on pink paper but assumes that it was sent to him from a forgiving wife, Mrs Cheveley having incompetently failed to indicate the addressee. So it seems that everything can be covered up again. When his wife tells him he is safe, his self-incriminating letter burnt (there is certainly a plethora of letters in the play), he even reverts momentarily to his old self-satisfaction. Has anything changed, we wonder, as he exults in his safety and wishes he could have seen the 'one sin' of his youth burning to ashes. Yet there has been a change. He made his speech without knowing that he was safe from retribution. And he is actually uneasy at not encountering any: he knows his wife and her puritanical expectations. Looking anxiously at her he asks, with one of those hesitations which are so significant in Wilde's dialogue, 'I suppose, Gertrude, . . . I suppose I should retire from public life?' Wilde shows that she has not yet learned her lesson; she has no hesitation in replying 'eagerly' that it is his duty to do so. With the promptness of the timing in a medieval morality play, Lord Caversham now appears, hot from the Prime Minister with the offer of a seat in the Cabinet which Chiltern is obliged to refuse, though it is made clear from his expression of 'triumph and joy' what his natural response would have been.

For the last time Lord Goring is called upon to play mentor and guardian angel to the Chilterns (a role the first actor of the part, Charles Hawtrey, failed to make convincing, according to Shaw). He tells his father, who is stupefied by Chiltern's reaction – 'What is the matter with the family? Something wrong here, eh? (tapping his forehead) Idiocy? Hereditary I suppose' – that it is 'what is called nowadays a high moral tone, father'. 'Hate these new-fangled names,' says Lord Caversham, 'same thing as we used to call idiocy fifty years ago.' It is droll, but in the scene that follows between Lord Goring and Lady Chiltern when he urges her not to rob her husband of the 'fruits of his ambition', we are told that Goring is making a great effort which reveals 'the philosopher who underlies the dandy'. It is Wilde's own philosophy of moderation and charity he expounds, though one must say, in regrettably chauvinist terms:

> Women are not meant to judge us, but to forgive us when we need forgiveness. Pardon, not punishment, is their mission . . . . A man's life is of more value than a woman's. It has larger issues, wider scope, greater ambitions.

A black mark for the debonair Lord Goring.

Perhaps it is the right sort of sermon for Lady Chiltern, however. She is not a subtle person, has not even realised that Sir Robert was making his gesture of renunciation entirely for her sake. But she sees her mistake in the end – 'I set him up too high' – and she responds to Goring's plea not to rob Chiltern of 'the splendour of a great political career' in a whole-hearted way, tearing up his letter of resignation with 'a gesture of passion'. 'Men easily forget', she says, with perhaps a touch of bitterness, 'and I forgive. That is how women help the world. I see that now.' She makes the bigger sacrifice, probably, for her husband does easily forget. In one of the most ironical turns in the play, Lord Goring's request for consent to his marriage with Mabel Chiltern is refused, with intense moral earnestness, on the ground that Chiltern 'cannot have her sacrificed'. There is some reason in this behaviour: he did discover Mrs Cheveley in Lord Goring's rooms and Goring did make an emotional speech which suggested that he was too involved with her to be a suitable husband for the young girl. Still the pharisaical tone is rather ludicrous in one whose feet of clay have been so recently exposed. Lady Chiltern must speak out, and she does, with a complete acceptance of her own faults and mistakes which, against the odds (and pace Shaw) surely wins at least a measure of sympathy for her at last.

The play moves to the happy ending which, as always in Wilde's comedies, is deeply equivocal. For Lord Goring and Mabel (and Lord Caversham, already established as the fondest of father-in-laws) the outlook is fine. We may see this couple as embodying Wilde's ideas on how to live life for the best. In this play, for the first time, the philosophy of love and tolerance is realised, through a witty, not a tragic figure. For the marriage of the Chilterns too Wilde holds out hope, though of a more dubious kind. In the final moment Sir Robert is left alone on the stage, brooding on his own inferiority, it seems, for when his wife comes back for him, he asks: 'Gertrude, is it love you feel for me, or is it pity merely?' She gives him a ringing assurance, on which the curtain falls: 'It is love, Robert,

Love, and only love. For both of us a new life is beginning.' Perhaps it is true: it is certainly the moral the play has been striving towards; a new life, the change of heart so much needed in both Chilterns, can only be brought about through love. Whether they will be able to sustain that new life is a very open question.

The critical reception of *An Ideal Husband* illustrates the curious range of responses Wilde's plays drew, even at the stage when he was immensely popular and well-established. There was often lack of understanding, accompanied by an extraordinarily patronising attitude toward the brilliance of his dialogue. It was in his review of *An Ideal Husband* (written after he had just become dramatic critic for the *Saturday Review*) that Shaw made his amusing remarks about the critics who 'protest that the trick is obvious, and that such epigrams can be turned out by the score by anyone lightminded enough to condescend to such frivolity'. One such was A. B. Walkley, who took the opportunity offered by the curious entangling of Wilde's and Henry James's theatrical fates, to write a review of odious comparisons. The situation was loaded with irony, for James's play, *Guy Domville*, was having its first night at the St James's (and being very ill received), while the nervous playwright was trying to distract himself by watching the first night of Wilde's play at the nearby Haymarket. 'He listened to the Oscarisms', says James's biographer, 'and was increasingly unnerved by the bursts of delighted laughter.' Rightly so, for when he returned to the St James's (Wilde's own theatre, one might say) and was brought on to the stage by a demoralised George Alexander, to take the author's call, he was greeted by boos. It was a total fiasco, for which James deserved sympathy: the kind he received from A. B. Walkley, however, was not much worth having, resting as it did on a ludicrously unfair comparison between James's play and *An Ideal Husband*, 'a strepitous, polychromatic, scintillant affair, dexterous as a conjuror's trick of legerdemain, clever with a cleverness so excessive as to be almost monstrous and uncanny'. *Guy Domville* had been 'despitefully' treated; yet, said Walkley, 'the brilliant success is infinitely outweighed by the ostensible failure'.[6]

It is the authentic voice of English philistinism, terrified by cleverness. It was left to two critics of greater percipience to argue on behalf of Wilde's 'monstrous' cleverness. William Archer, as a dour Scotsman, had some reservations about Wilde's pyrotechnics but he continually emphasised Wilde's intellectual achievement in the play. And Shaw, though taking a line of interpretation which was not quite Wilde's own, had no doubt that *An Ideal Husband* was a work of intellect which raised the level of theatre in England: 'The six worst epigrams are mere alms handed with a kind smile to the average suburban playgoer; the three best remain secrets between Mr Wilde and a few choice spirits.' He revelled in the Irishness which made Wilde, like Shaw himself, such an ironic observer of English phlegm: '. . . to the Irishman (and Mr Wilde is almost as acutely Irish an Irishman as the Iron Duke of Wellington), there is nothing in the world quite so exquisitely comic as an Englishman's seriousness.' The audience, suggested Shaw, could not help being amused, and was annoyed at being amused; shocked, really, at 'the danger to the foundations of society when seriousness is publicly laughed at'. This was the vein to be explored – more fully than anyone had done before or has done since – in Wilde's next play.

8
'The Importance of Being Earnest'

First performed St James's Theatre, 14 February 1895.
Published 1899 (in limited edition).

The Importance of Being Earnest is Wilde's funniest play
and it is also the most poignant, if we have in mind – as
how can we not? – the disaster that struck its author only a
few weeks after its glittering first night when Queensberry
instigated the process that led to Reading Gaol. It was just
the terrible peripeteia he had imagined for Robert
Chiltern: one moment the 'splendid position', the next,
public humiliation and the odious gloating of hypocrites.
The fall was symbolically encapsulated in the fate of the
posters advertising the new play and also *An Ideal
Husband* which was still running at the Haymarket. A splendid position indeed, to have two plays enjoying huge success
side by side in London's most fashionable theatres. Yet it
was wiped out overnight, when Wilde's name was

obliterated from the posters, by George Alexander at the St James's, and Lewis Waller at the Haymarket. It is something to set against the weakness of the two actors, who owed so much to Wilde, the courage of Charles Wyndham who refused to receive *An Ideal Husband* at his theatre, the Criterion (where it had been scheduled to move), unless Wilde's name were restored to the bills. And this was done.

In *The Importance of Being Earnest* the pleasure principle at last enjoys complete triumph. Some critics disapprove of this, notably Mary McCarthy who censures the dandies' determination to live a life of pleasure as 'selfishness'.[1] Perhaps it is, but we are not being required to examine their moral behaviour in humane Chekhovian terms. This is a philosophical farce, an existential farce, to use the modern term which modern criticism is beginning to see as appropriate for this witty exploration of identities. 'Pleasure', a word which recurs much, is a shorthand for the idea Wilde expounded in 'The Soul of Man under Socialism':

> Pleasure is Nature's test, her sign of approval. When man is happy, he is in harmony with himself and his environment. The new Individualism, for whose service Socialism, whether it wills it or not, is working, will be perfect harmony.[2]

Only in Utopia can this harmony be achieved; in theatrical terms that meant farce, the form that refused the agonies of melodrama. Wilde had observed that farce and burlesque offered the artist in England more freedom than the 'higher' forms of drama. He was following Nietzsche, who had said much the same thing a decade or so earlier.

153

In this extravagant genre, which no one took seriously, the dionysiac spirit could be fully released, to overturn respectable reality, and through paradox, fantasy and contradiction establish a logic of its own, defying the censorious super-ego. As Wilde put it in an interview given before the first production, the philosophy of his piece is that 'we should treat all the trivial things of life very seriously and all the serious things of life with sincere and studied triviality'.[3] It is a play of mirror images in which ordinary, everyday life can still be glimpsed through the comic distortions imposed upon it. Everything is double, from the double life of Algernon and Jack to the sets of doubles at the end, when the girls form themselves into opposition to the male image which has so conspicuously failed to be 'Ernest'.

In this play more than in any of the others it is vital for the actors to seem unaware of the absurdity of what they do and say. In the first production Irene Vanbrugh, playing Gwendolen, was paralysed with terror at being unable to find the right style; someone advised her to 'think' the lines before speaking them, and she felt she then became more natural. However, according to Shaw, the actors in the first production were insufferably affected: Cecily had too much conscious charm, the older ladies too much low comedy; even George Alexander, whose grave, refined manner as Jack made suitable contrast with Algernon's easy-going style, ruined the third act by bustling through at such a rate that he quite lost the 'subdued earnestness' which Shaw felt should characterise the role.[4] (Wilde had doubted his suitability for the part.) A few years later (in the 1902 revival at the St James's) Max Beerbohm found the actors making the same mistakes. Only Lilian Braithwaite 'in seeming to take her part quite seriously, showed that she had realised the full extent of its fun'. George Alexander was still bustling – at breakneck speed – and the part of Chasuble was played 'as though it were a minutely realistic character study of the typical country clergyman'.[5]

'Everything matters in art except the subject,' said Wilde. In *The Importance of Being Earnest* the subject certainly cannot be distinguished from the style, yet the fact that the play succeeded (as it did on both the occasions quoted) even when the actors were playing it wrongly shows what a steely construction it has. It must have given Wilde the craftsman much pleasure to take the familiar melodrama mechanism (mistaken identities, incriminating inscriptions, secrets of the past) and exploit its inherent absurdity instead of trying to restrain it. The closeness of farce to melodrama is one of his strong cards, in fact, allowing all kinds of oblique references to the oppressive moral laws which had malign consequences in the earlier plays – and, as Wilde thought, in English society. As well as being an existential farce, *The Importance of Being Earnest* is his supreme demolition of late nineteenth-century social and moral attitudes, the triumphal conclusion to his career as revolutionary moralist.

Wilde has sometimes been seen as an over-tolerant, even careless craftsman, only too ready to accept textual alterations called for by his actor-managers. *The Importance of Being Earnest* has been cited as an illustration: it was originally in the more usual four-act form, but when Alexander asked him to shorten it (almost unbelievably, to make room for a curtain raiser) Wilde obliged him to the extent of dropping the third act. As Lady Bracknell might have said, to lose a scene or two might be regarded as a misfortune, to lose a whole act seems like carelessness. However, if we study the four-act draft, we can see how far from carelessly Wilde made his revisions and indeed how much the play is improved by rigorous cutting which gives it a more spare and modern look.[6] Farce should have the speed of a pistol shot, said Wilde, and speed is, indeed, a distinctive and curious feature of *The Importance of Being Earnest*; curious, because it co-exists with extreme slowness and stateliness in the dialogue. No one is ever so agitated that he cannot take time to round a sentence, find the right metaphor – or finish off the last muffin. Yet all the time sensational changes are occurring at the speed of light. Proposals of marriage are found to have been received even before they were uttered, relations lost and found before one can say 'hand-bag'. Time, like everything else, goes double and through the 'gaps' Wilde insinuates the notion that the action is really all happening somewhere else, in the mental dimension where ruling fantasies are conceived, which is not to say of course that there is no connection with reality: 'Life imitates Art far more than Art imitates life.' The outlines of reality are easily discernible; Lane offering deadpan excuses for the absence of cucumber sandwiches, Dr Chasuble fitting in the absurd christening to his perfectly normal programme: 'In fact I have two similar ceremonies to perform at that time. A case of twins that occurred recently in one of the outlying cottages on your own estate. Poor Jenkins the carter, a most hard-working man.' What is wrong with this society, so the farce implies, is its fatal inability to distinguish between the trivial and the serious. Sense and nonsense, reason and fantasy, facts and truth, are juggled with, forcing new perspectives, offering release from the cramp of habit and logic:

> ALGERNON: Please don't touch the cucumber sandwiches. They are ordered specially for Aunt Augusta. (*Takes one and eats it*.)

JACK: Well, you have been eating them all the time.

ALGERNON: That is quite a different matter. She is my aunt.

How can one challenge the impeccable logic of this? Only by lapsing into earnestness, which the play is set up expressly to forbid. Shaw's complaint that the farce was never lifted onto a higher plane was an extraordinary failure of judgment for him. How good-humoured of Wilde to say only 'I am disappointed in you'.

It is an urbane vision we see when the curtain goes up on the first act. Algernon's rooms in Half Moon Street (a more relaxed environment than the grand locales of earlier plays) are 'luxuriously and artistically furnished'; music is heard from the off-stage piano (perhaps a dubious pleasure, as Algernon saves his science for life and relies on sentiment in his piano playing). The elegant sallies between Algernon and his 'ideal butler', Lane, are another feature of Wilde's Utopia; servants are more than equal to masters. With the entrance of Jack, the 'pleasure' motif rings out loud and clear:

ALGERNON: How are you, my dear Ernest? What brings you up to town?

JACK: Oh pleasure, pleasure! What else should bring one anywhere . . .

Tom Stoppard lifted this debonair entrance to serve as a 'time stop' in *Travesties*, a sticking place in the mind to which the action obsessively returns. He assigns Jack's lines to Tristan Tzara, the Dadaist, making a connection between the pleasure philosophy, revolution and nihilism. Jack and Algernon are not exactly revolutionaries, but they do bring into the play from time to time a rather modern emphasis on the idea of nothingness, as when they discuss ways they might spend the evening:

> ALGERNON: What shall we do after dinner? Go to a theatre?
> JACK: Oh no! I loathe listening.
> ALGERNON: Well, let us go to the Club?
> JACK: Oh no! I hate talking.
> ALGERNON: Well, we might trot round to the Empire at ten?
> JACK: Oh no! I can't bear looking at things. It is so silly.
> ALGERNON: Well, what shall we do?
> JACK: Nothing!

The malaise is kept at bay most of the time by the complications of the double life. Wilde amusingly recalls the impassioned detective sequences of *An Ideal Husband* in the inquisition conducted by Algernon into Jack's secrets. A precious mislaid object, the inscribed cigarette case, provides a crucial clue (parallelling the bracelet/brooch of the other play); Algernon presses his questions as unremittingly as Lady Chiltern ('But why does she call you little Cecily, if she is your aunt and lives at Tunbridge Wells?') and like Robert Chiltern, Jack fights off discovery with inventive lies. 'Earnest' was the word for the Chiltern double life and 'Earnest' is the word for Jack's too, in the double sense perceived by Algernon the moment Jack reveals his 'real' name:

> ALGERNON: . . . Besides, your name isn't Jack at all; it is Ernest.
> JACK: It isn't Ernest; it's Jack.
> ALGERNON: You have always told me it was Ernest. I have introduced you to everyone as Ernest. You answer to the name of Ernest. You look as if your

name is Ernest. You are the most earnest-looking
person I ever saw in my life.

The brilliant pun is the corner-stone of a structure
dedicated to dualities of all kinds. Jack is 'Ernest in town
and Jack in the country': he becomes 'Ernest' in fact when
he wants to escape from being 'earnest'; the pun perfectly
encapsulates the split in the personality. Neatness, taken to
the point of surrealist absurdity, makes the same sort of
suggestion throughout. Algernon's situation is a mirror
image of Jack's. When he sums up the situation, he falls
into a rhythm which is the quintessential rhythm of the
play; a balancing of opposites, the 'masks', which as the
play goes on are to be juggled with increasingly manic
ingenuity:

> You have invented a very useful younger brother called
> Ernest in order that you may be able to come up to town
> as often as you like. I have invented an invaluable
> permanent invalid called Bunbury, in order that I may
> be able to go down into the country whenever I choose.

Critics in Wilde's time did not grasp the subtlety of the
structure. Even Max Beerbohm, an admirer, thought the
play triumphed despite its farcical 'scheme' which he
summarised as: 'the story of a young man coming up to
London "on the spree", and of another young man going
down conversely to the country, and of the complications
that ensue'. This comes nowhere near expressing the
mysterious sense of what 'town' and 'country' represent
for Jack and Algernon. 'On the spree' is a phrase for the
French *boulevard* farce and its 'naughty' behaviour, which
English audiences could enjoy in suitably watered down
adaptations, with a feeling of moral superiority. Wilde

slyly draws attention to this characteristic hypocrisy when Algernon gives Jack some very French advice:

ALGERNON: A man who marries without knowing Bunbury has a very tedious time of it.

JACK: That is nonsense. If I marry a charming girl like Gwendolen, and she is the only girl I ever saw in my life that I would marry, I certainly won't want to know Bunbury.

ALGERNON: Then your wife will. You don't seem to realise, that in married life three is company and two is none.

JACK (*sententiously*): That, my dear young friend, is the theory that the corrupt French Drama has been propounding for the last fifty years.

ALGERNON: Yes; and that the happy English home has proved in half the time.

There is little sense in the play of orgiastic goings on. 'Eating' is the chief symbol of sensual activity.[7] The dandies' will to eat is part of the larger will which drives them and the girls (and indeed everyone in the play). Shaw might have called it the Life Force. Wilde uses a favourite metaphor: health. As Jack explains to Algernon, he needs Ernest because as Uncle Jack he is expected to maintain a high moral tone, and a high moral tone can hardly be said to conduce to one's health or happiness. We might wonder why the insouciant Algernon needs an escape route. But we find out when Lady Bracknell appears on the scene, ringing the bell in 'Wagnerian manner' and greeting her nephew in a most remarkable variant of common usage: 'I hope you are behaving very well?' He fights back with 'I'm feeling very well, Aunt Augusta', only to be overridden with magisterial finality: 'That is not quite the same thing. In fact the two rarely go together.' Judi Dench's unusually youthful Lady Bracknell in the National Theatre's 1982 production clearly had a somewhat over-fond interest in her elegant nephew, an unexpected slant which increased the psychological interest (Peter Hall, directing, saw the play as being 'about love and about reality').

Lady Bracknell herself is dedicated to health; a supreme irony. As she tells Algernon when he produces Bunbury's illness yet again, as an excuse for avoiding her dinner party:

> I think it is high time that Mr Bunbury made up his mind whether he was going to live or to die. This shilly-shallying with the question is absurd. Nor do I in any way approve of the modern sympathy with invalids. I consider it morbid. Illness of any kind is hardly a thing to be encouraged in others. Health is the primary duty of life . . .

We can well see why Lord Bracknell had to become an invalid: she has taken all the health for herself. It is a measure of Wilde's ability to stand back from his own passionately held beliefs that the most completely realised personality in the play should be such a monster; as Jack says, 'a monster without being a myth, which is rather unfair'.

There is no doubt in this play that 'women rule society'. Lady Bracknell has a more central position in the dramatic action than the dowagers of earlier plays. The marriages are in her control, and it is she who (unwittingly) holds the key to Jack's identity. She comes on with Gwendolen in tow, in the manner of the Duchess of Berwick and Lady

Agatha, and though Gwendolen is no Agatha, she is just as much in thrall to her mother when husbands are in question. On one of its levels the farce is certainly conducting the old campaign against the tyrannies that afflict women. There is an extra layer of irony indeed; we see how the system will perpetuate itself as the victims prepare to become tyrants in their turn, for Gwendolen is clearly her mother's daughter. It is not just a joke when Jack anxiously enquires: 'You don't think there is any chance of Gwendolen becoming like her mother in about a hundred and fifty years, do you, Algy?' The proposal scene certainly gives him warning, with its focus on Gwendolen's will and the intensity of the inner life which surfaces (in appropriately 'absurd' form) in her curious obsession:

> My ideal has always been to love someone of the name of Ernest. There is something in that name that inspires absolute confidence. The moment Algernon first mentioned to me that he had a friend called Ernest, I knew I was destined to love you.

There is obviously a dig here at the troublesome idealists of earlier plays: the whole ideal-oriented ethos is reduced to absurdity. It is a philosophical as well as a social joke, however. Could she not love him if he had some other name? 'Ah!' says Gwendolen, 'that is clearly a metaphysical speculation, and like most metaphysical speculations has very little reference at all to the actual facts of real life as we know them.' She says it 'glibly'; that is Wilde's joke, for though Gwendolen may be intellectually shallow, her devotion to her 'ideal' reflects concepts Wilde took very seriously. Gwendolen is making the sacred effort to 'realise one's own personality on some imaginative plane out of reach of the trammelling accidents and limitations of real life'. When Jack calls her 'perfect' she resists the term: 'It would leave no room for developments, and I intend to develop in many directions.'

The 'limitations of real life' are soon imposed on the idyll when Lady Bracknell sweeps in, to surprise Jack on his knees: 'Rise, sir, from this semi-recumbent posture. It is most indecorous.' Her marriage questionnaire carries, in its absurd way, the whole weight of the commercially-minded society she epitomises:

LADY BRACKNELL: . . . What is your income?

JACK: Between seven and eight thousand a year.

LADY BRACKNELL (*makes a note in her book*): In land, or in investments?

JACK: In investments, chiefly.

LADY BRACKNELL: That is satisfactory. What between the duties expected of one during one's lifetime, and the duties exacted from one after one's death, land has ceased to be either a profit or a pleasure. It gives one position, and prevents one from keeping it up. That's all that can be said about land.

Anyone who can talk as well as this is bound to charm – still she cannot be thought totally charming. Real life is hovering there in the background, making us feel just a little mean at laughing when she holds forth on the nature of society from the height of her conservative hauteur. Her power is political as well as social; Wilde's point is that the two are one. Liberal Unionists are acceptable, she concedes, when Jack admits to being one: 'they count as Tories. They dine with us. Or come in the evenings, at any rate.' The fine shades of her condescension are droll, but a telling reminder of a real-life Byzantine grading system which ensures that politics are controlled by the right people.

It does not really matter what Jack admits to in the way of taste: there is no way of kowtowing to Lady Bracknell, for, as Mary McCarthy says, she has the unpredictability of a thorough *grande dame*. Jack is no doubt taken aback, as we are, by the remarkable triviality of her first question – 'Do you smoke?' – and no doubt equally surprised by her response to his admission that he does:

> I am glad to hear it. A man should always have an occupation of some kind. There are far too many idle men in London as it is.

It makes him understandably wary when she declares that 'a man who desires to get married should know either everything or nothing', and asks 'which' he knows. It is only 'after some hesitation' that he commits himself: 'I know nothing, Lady Bracknell.' A fitting remark for an existential hero. She, of course, takes it in a social sense, as she does everything, and approves; a rich irony, for Jack's devotion to 'nothing' goes along with his mercurial changeability, something she would deeply disapprove of. 'Knowing nothing' for her means 'ignorance', a very desirable quality in the lower classes:

> The whole theory of modern education is radically unsound. Fortunately in England, at any rate, education produces no effect whatsoever. If it did, it would prove a serious danger to the upper classes, and probably lead to acts of violence in Grosvenor Square.

Great fun, in the context, yet are we meant to quite shut out reverberations from history – the Nihilists, the Irish, all the social ferment which troubled Wilde's conscience and is reflected in his other plays? It seems not, for the revolution theme comes up again in an explicit historical reference when Jack reveals the peculiar circumstances of his birth. Even Lady Bracknell cannot assimilate that anarchical phenomenon:

> . . . I don't actually know who I am by birth. I was . . . well, I was found . . . In a hand-bag – a somewhat large, black, leather hand-bag, with handles to it . . .

All her worst nightmares crowd – majestically – into the scene:

> To be born, or at any rate bred, in a hand-bag, whether it had handles or not, seems to me to display a contempt for the ordinary decencies of family life that reminds one of the worst excesses of the French Revolution. And I presume you know what that unfortunate movement led to?

This is no casual reference. The French Revolution figures in 'The Soul of Man under Socialism' as illustration of the inevitability of change: 'The systems that fail are those that rely on the permanency of human nature, and not on its growth and development. The error of Louis XIV was that he thought that human nature would always be the same. The result of his error was the French Revolution. It was an admirable result.' By analogy, Lady Bracknell is necessary to the process she is resisting; Wilde provides us with a moral justification for the fact that we cannot help liking the monster!

There is also a little germ of existential anxiety in the great joke: 'being' in an empty hand-bag; being in a void.

Like a Vladimir or a Winnie in Beckett's empty spaces, Jack has to construct himself from virtually nothing. That is more or less what Lady Bracknell advises him to do before she departs in high dudgeon at the idea of Gwendolen being asked to 'marry into a cloak-room, and form an alliance with a parcel'. 'I would strongly advise you, Mr Worthing,' she says, 'to try and acquire some relations as soon as possible.' Ridiculous, yet it has already happened. Younger brother Ernest is soon to acquire extraordinary reality. Jack's fertile imagination rises to these challenges. 'Gwendolen, I must get christened at once,' was his immediate reaction to the revelation that she could only love a man called Ernest.

At the fall of the curtain on the first act the metaphysical dimension is thickening. Jack is in a tortuous relationship with the mythic self which he needs both to destroy ('I am going to kill my brother') and at the same time possess more completely (by having himself christened, a comical psychic ordeal). And Algernon, with the address of 'excessively pretty Cecily' surreptitiously registered on his shirt-cuff, is gleefully preparing to get into his Bunbury clothes and take over the adaptable 'Ernest' identity for himself. The juggling with personae is becoming more and more 'absurd' in the modern sense.

The second act opens in a garden, a natural setting such as Wilde had never quite allowed himself in earlier plays where the furthest we got into nature was a lawn under a terrace (though one critic draws attention to garden imagery in the dialogue of *A Woman of No Importance*).[8] This is not very wild nature, of course: still, there is emphasis on luxuriance (an old-fashioned abundance of roses) and various hints that this is the scene where growth and change are to be achieved. The 'blue glass' stage floor and cut-out garden accessories in Peter

Hall's 1982 production struck the right note of artfully stylised simplicity. In the four-act version a gardener appeared, an unexpected addition to the usual cast of butlers and valets. Here Cecily (significantly seen at the back of the stage, deep in the garden) is doing the gardener's work, a fact Miss Prism observes with distaste:

> MISS PRISM (*calling*): Cecily, Cecily! Surely such a utilitarian occupation as the watering of flowers is rather Moulton's duty than yours? Especially at a moment when intellectual pleasures await you. Your German grammar is on the table. Pray open it at page fifteen. We will repeat yesterday's lesson.
>
> CECILY (*coming over very slowly*): But I don't like German. It isn't at all a becoming language. I know perfectly well that I look quite plain after my German lesson.

The reference to German as the bone of contention is no accident. Like the 'pessimist' joke at the close of act one (Algernon accuses Lane of being a pessimist and is told 'I always endeavour to give satisfaction, sir'), it is one of those oblique allusions to German philosophy which slyly suggest that the characters are enacting a Schopenhauer style struggle to realise the 'will' and engage with the concept of 'nothing'. Jack always lays particular stress on the importance of Cecily's German when he goes off to town (to become his alter ego). So Miss Prism observes, while Cecily notes the strain involved: 'Dear Uncle Jack is so very serious! Sometimes he is so serious that I think he cannot be quite well.' She draws attention to the existential confusion which surely overtakes the audience by now. Who really is Jack/Ernest? Is he acting when he is serious Uncle Jack and is Ernest his true identity (as Gwendolen asserts)? Or is he really Jack struggling to manage the wicked brother, Ernest? He is often half way between the two, as the fluctuations in his style indicate. The man who entered the play on so airy a note ('Oh, pleasure, pleasure!') can talk very sententiously, and look the part too, as Algernon had observed.

Cecily has no such complications. Yet she is also in her way an existentialist, using her diary as the young men use Ernest to act out her 'will'. Wilde strikes very modern notes in the discussion sparked off by the diary about the difficulty of distinguishing between memory and fiction, both seen here as part of the self-creating process:

> CECILY: I keep a diary in order to enter the wonderful secrets of my life. If I didn't write them down, I should probably forget all about them.
> MISS PRISM: Memory, my dear Cecily, is the diary that we all carry about with us.
> CECILY: Yes, but it usually chronicles the things that have never happened, and couldn't possibly have happened. I believe that Memory is responsible for nearly all the three-volume novels that Mudie sends us.

Miss Prism's confession that she once wrote a three-volume novel (leading to her memorable definition: 'The good ended happily, and the bad unhappily. That is what Fiction means') contributes to the Beckettian shades in the comedy. But she, like her other half, Canon Chasuble, is really essence of nineteenth century. Through their delicious absurdities we discern, like shadows, characteristics that had to be taken more grimly in earlier plays: pomposity, self-importance, cruelty even (Miss Prism is much given to pronouncing 'As a man sows, so also shall he reap'). But rigid morality loses its power when the absurdly serious pair represent it. They have a foot in the utopian world.

Miss Prism too pursues a dream: 'You are too much alone, dear Dr Chasuble. You should get married. A misanthrope I can understand – a womanthrope, never!' His scholarly shudder at the 'neologistic' phrase reminds us, like his reference to Egeria which Miss Prism fails to understand ('My name is Laetitia, Doctor'), that there is a social gulf between them. She is hardly a highly-educated governess; we learn later that she started life as a nursemaid. Wilde is extending the satire on Victorian moral attitudes to take in the middle to lower classes, an interesting development which makes one more than ever sad at what may have been lost when catastrophe brought his playwriting to an end.

Cecily soon clears the stage for her own freedom. In her manipulation of the wobbling celibates ('it would do her so much good to have a short stroll with you in the park, Dr Chasuble'), she displays the masterfulness which makes her, like Gwendolen, more than a match for the men. Like a modern girl, she cuts Algernon down to size when he makes his appearance as Ernest on a somewhat arch note:

ALGERNON: You are my little cousin, Cecily, I'm sure.
CECILY: You are under some strange mistake. I am not little. In fact, I believe I am more than usually tall for my age.

Algernon, says the stage direction, is 'rather taken aback'. Well he might be: it is the end of his Bunburying days when Cecily takes charge, leading him into the house to start the process of 'reforming' him.

Oscar Wilde

It is an exquisite stroke of comic timing that at the very moment when brother Ernest has materialised for the first time, Jack should enter, in mourning for his death in Paris of a chill. Pictures of George Alexander in the part show him the very spirit of lugubriousness, in funereal black, with the 'crepe hatband and black gloves' which Dr Chasuble calls his 'garb of woe'. It is a great visual joke, demonstrating, as C. E. Montague said, the scenic imagination which distinguishes playwrights from other writers: 'To an audience, knowing what it knows, the mere first sight of those black clothes is convulsingly funny; it is a visible stroke of humour, a witticism not heard but seen.'[9] Wilde did not make much of the stage directions for *The Importance of Being Earnest*: they are less detailed than in earlier plays. When preparing proofs for publication in 1899, he remarked to Robert Ross that he did not much like giving physical details 'about the bodies whose souls, or minds, or passions, I deal with. I build up so much out of *words* that the colour of people's hair seems unimportant.' Yet Montague was right to stress the value of the scenic element. We do not need to know the colour of the characters' hair – what colour would Ernest's be? – but, as in all the plays, a delicate visual symbolism operates in *The Importance of Being Earnest*, crystallising underlying meanings. The spectacle of the 'man in black' making those absurd arrangements to be christened ('Ah, that reminds me, you mentioned christenings, I think, Dr Chasuble?') is surely, for us now, an existential joke.

Of course none of this shows to the stage audience. Jack's rather disturbing fluidity of character is highlighted by the rigidity of Miss Prism and Canon Chasuble: they move on the narrowest of lines and appeal to our sense of humour by having none themselves. It is one of Wilde's most dionysiac moments of glee when Jack, acting solemnity, draws forth the real solemnity of the celibate pair:

> CHASUBLE: Was the cause of death mentioned?
> JACK: A severe chill, it seems.
> MISS PRISM: As a man sows, so shall he reap.
> CHASUBLE (*raising his hand*): Charity, dear Miss Prism, charity! None of us are perfect. I myself am peculiarly susceptible to draughts. Will the interment take place here?
> JACK: No. He seems to have expressed a desire to be buried in Paris.
> CHASUBLE: In Paris! (*shakes his head*) I fear that hardly points to any very serious state of mind at the last.

This is the sort of caricature which is more lifelike than life itself. The consistent pair are in their way an anchor to a solid world where we expect people to be much the same from one day to another. In the other dimension, where there seems no limit to the characters' ability to change themselves, the action is becoming manic:

> My brother is in the dining-room? I don't know what it all means. I think it is perfectly absurd.

It is 'absurd' in Pinteresque vein when Jack, in mourning for Ernest, is impudently advised to 'change':

> Why on earth don't you go up and change? It is perfectly childish to be in deep mourning for a man who is actually staying for a whole week with you in your house as a guest. I call it grotesque.

The alter ego is out of hand. Even the imperturbable

Algernon is taken aback, in his second scene with Cecily, to realise how firmly she has defined his role in her 'girlish dream'. It was 'on the 14th of February last that worn out by your entire ignorance of my existence, I determined to end the matter one way or the other, and after a long struggle with myself I accepted you under this dear old tree here.' A very determined piece of dreaming, this, – a comical version of Schopenhauer's 'world as idea' – held together, like Gwendolen's scenario, by the 'ideal' Ernest.

Repetition and increasingly heavy stylisation from now on build up the impression that some psychic process is being acted out – in the absurd form appropriate to events in the unconscious. Algernon and Cecily must go through the same performance as Jack and Gwendolen; he must react in the same way as Jack to the realisation that 'Ernest' is no longer a voluntary role by rushing off to be christened. And Gwendolen must appear, for a quarrel scene with Cecily which is in a way closer to the norm of nineteenth century comedy (Gilbert's *Engaged* was mentioned by contemporary critics), but acquires strangeness from the dream-like gap Wilde contrives between the solid, decorous surface (Merriman totally absorbed in supervising the tea-table rites) and the increasingly uninhibited argument about someone who doesn't exist. As the lines become ever more crossed – 'Oh, but it is not Mr Ernest Worthing who is my guardian. It is his brother – his elder brother' – the audience has almost certainly lost its own grip on who is who, a confusion Wilde surely intends.

He evidently intends also the exaggerated stylisation which begins to push the farce away from even minimal realism when Jack and Algernon are brought face to face with Gwendolen and Cecily. Like automata, the girls ask the same questions and use the same movements, each in turn demanding of 'her' Ernest, 'May I ask if you are engaged to be married to this young lady?', and on receiving the desired assurance, proceeding to prick the bubble of the other's dream with a mannered precision which has drawn from modern critics terms like 'courtship dance' to describe the manoeuvrings of the quartet:

> The gentleman whose arm is at present round your waist is my guardian, Mr John Worthing.

> The gentleman who is now embracing you is my cousin, Mr Algernon Moncrieff.

The breaking up and re-forming of pairs, the neat oppositions, the stilted repetitions, the speaking for each other (Gwendolen takes over Cecily's unformed question, 'Where is your brother Ernest?'); all create a curious impression, of personality flowing unstoppably between two poles. Everything surprises us by being its own opposite ('A truth in Art is that whose contradictory is also true'). Things taken with deadly seriousness in the 'modern life' plays are stood on their head, as in Jack's parodic confession:

> Gwendolen – Cecily – it is very painful for me to be forced to speak the truth. It is the first time in my life I have ever been reduced to such a painful position, and I am really quite inexperienced in doing anything of the kind. However I will tell you quite frankly that I have no brother Ernest . . . .

A subtle joke; for by the end we know that his brilliant invention was the truth; it was the facts that were untrustworthy ('Life imitates art far more than art imitates life').

Before we arrive at that revelation, the doubles have to reorganise themselves. The female pair retire into the house 'with scornful looks' and the male pair are left to pick up the pieces of the shattered personality. Time is going round in circles; we are almost back in the first act with the cucumber sandwiches when Algernon settles down to the muffins and Jack reproaches him: 'How you can sit there calmly eating muffins, when we are in this horrible trouble, I can't make out. You seem to me to be perfectly heartless.' Never for him, it seems, the intellectual aplomb which allows Algernon to short-circuit 'absurd' anxieties with absurd and unanswerable logic: 'Well, I can't eat muffins in an agitated manner. The butter would probably get on my cuffs.'

In the final act we move back into the house; the garden idyll (the 'beautiful' act, Wilde called it) is over, the 'truth' is out and time is flowing back towards daylight. Gwendolen and Cecily are seen looking out of the windows at the young men, as if no time at all has elapsed, or just enough for them to say, in the past tense, 'they have been eating muffins'. Stylisation reaches its peak when the young men join them and both pairs address each other in choral unison, Gwendolen beating time 'with uplifted finger'. In an early draft, this went on longer and lines were split between characters; as Russell Jackson says, accentuating the effect of a duet.[10] It is an altogether musical scene: the men come on whistling 'some dreadful popular air from a British opera' (not identified, but could Wilde wickedly have intended *Patience*?). In earlier drafts the stylisation was even more extreme and balletic. Jack and Algernon were to 'move together like Siamese twins in every movement' when they make their announcement that they are to be christened:

First to front of sofa, then fold hands together, then raise eyes to ceiling, then sit on sofa, unfold hands, lean back, tilting up legs with both feet off the ground, then twitch trousers above knee à la dude . . .

It is almost surrealist farce now; Jarry's painted puppets are over the horizon, and Ionesco's automata chorusing 'The future is in eggs'. Directors, alas, seldom pick up Wilde's hints for a modern style; they tend to keep a uniform tone, ignoring the upsurge of stylisation that makes the characters speak in tune, whistle, chant in chorus until, symmetrical to the last, the pairs are reconciled and fall into each other's arms, exclaiming 'Darling!'.

Only if this fantastic, balletic/musical effect is achieved (Peter Hall's production went further in this direction than most), can there be the right contrast of tone when Lady Bracknell sweeps in to drag them back to the real world. Despite the fun, that is what is happening when she sets about demolishing one unsuitable engagement and investigating the other with the suspicion induced by the previous day's revelations. 'Until yesterday I had no idea that there were any families or persons whose origin was a Terminus.' The wit warms us to her but cannot quite disguise the glacial nature of the snub. The whole tone is harder in this scene, perhaps because she is ruder (she makes Jack 'perfectly furious' and 'very irritable'); perhaps because repetition slightly reduces the comicality of her routines, making their social unpleasantness more apparent. When she asks 'as a matter of form' if Cecily has any fortune and on learning that she has a hundred and thirty thousand pounds in the Funds, finds her 'a most attractive young lady', we laugh, of course, but remembering the similar business with Jack, probably feel the edge in the joke more. There is something increasingly alarming as well as droll about her unselfconsciousness: can she really be so unaware or impervious, we wonder, or is she amusing herself with conscious irony when she reflects on Cecily's 'really solid qualities' and how they will 'last and improve with time', and with supreme effrontery presents herself as the opponent of mercenary marriages:

> Dear child, of course you know that Algernon has nothing but his debts to depend on. But I do not approve of mercenary marriages. When I married Lord Bracknell I had no fortune of any kind. But I never dreamed for a moment of allowing that to stand in my way.

There is no way of penetrating that formidable façade, to find out what goes on behind it (Peter Hall saw the whole action as determined by the will to conceal very strong and real feelings). Wilde planted a time bomb in this character, seemingly set for our time, when there would be a better chance of audiences picking up the serious points the jokes are making – about the 'woman question' and marriage. The revelation that Cecily remains a ward till she is thirty-five, for instance, yields much fun, culminating in Lady Bracknell's dry comment that her reluctance to wait till then to be married shows 'a somewhat impatient nature'. Yet there are sour realities at the back of it, which Wilde does not mean to go unnoticed: we are laughing at (laughing down?) the idea of women being always someone's property, always pawns in the marriage business. Lady Bracknell has made it grotesquely clear that 'business' is the word, and she controls society. It is total impasse – the only way out in the other dimension, where Ernest has his equivocal being.

That unpredictable force makes its way back when

Canon Chasuble appears, unctuously announcing that he is ready to perform the christenings. It is a wonderful clash of the two worlds. 'Algernon, I forbid you to be baptised,' booms Lady Bracknell: 'Lord Bracknell would be highly displeased if he learned that that was the way in which you wasted your time and money.' But the materialist money values, so comically invoked, must give way before the strange inner drive that dictated the christenings; now it brings on Miss Prism, in anxious pursuit of the Canon ('I was told you expected me in the vestry, dear Canon') to be confronted with Lady Bracknell's stony glare and the terrible question: 'Prism! Where is that baby?' The absurd tale of the three-volume novel left in the perambulator and the baby left in the hand-bag closely parodies attitudes taken in Wilde's other plays. Miss Prism 'bows her head in shame', the young men 'pretend' to protect the girls from hearing 'the details of a terrible public scandal', Jack becomes ever more portentous, requiring Miss Prism to examine *his* hand-bag carefully to see if it is also hers: 'The happiness of more than one life depends on your answer.' The third act was 'abominably clever', Wilde said. Nothing is cleverer than the way he uses the individualism of his characters to undermine the old attitudes, overturn them, indeed, by being irresistibly themselves. Miss Prism cannot keep her head down for long: one sight of the hand-bag, and she is away in her own world where other things, like damage to the lining, are far more important than a sense of shame:

. . . here is the injury it received through the upsetting of a Gower Street omnibus in younger and happier days. Here is the stain on the lining caused by the explosion of a temperance beverage, an incident that occurred at Leamington . . . . The bag is undoubtedly mine. I am delighted to have it so unexpectedly restored to me. It has been a great inconvenience being without it all these years.

No melodrama morality could survive the absurdity of this. Wilde rolls the whole drama of the 'woman with a past', the seduced victim, the illegitimate child (one critic would include the idea of incest), into the tiny hilarious episode when Jack tries to embrace Miss Prism, taking her for his mother. She recoils, exclaiming that she is unmarried, and he makes his sentimental declaration: 'Unmarried! I do not deny that is a serious blow. But after all, who has the right to cast a stone against one who has suffered? Cannot repentance wipe out an act of folly? Why should there be one law for men and another for women? Mother, I forgive you.'

Laughing at himself, as well as at the mores of his time, Wilde in this scene breaks quite free of his century and becomes the 'modern' playwright he wished to be. It is a modern moment for an audience brought up on Pirandello and Beckett when Jack, turning from one character to another in search of the truth about himself, is directed by Miss Prism to Lady Bracknell – 'There is the lady who can tell you who you really are' – and asks her the question that has been causing existential tremors throughout the play: '. . . Would you kindly inform me who I am?' The answer may be something we have seen coming but still it causes a shock and it is not purely comic; it is bound to be a little disturbing to find that his wild and seemingly casual invention was no more than the truth: he is the brother of Algernon and his name is Ernest.

The existential hero receives the news 'quite calmly' – 'I always said I had a brother! Cecily, – how could you have ever doubted that I had a brother?; 'I always told you, Gwendolen, my name was Ernest . . .' But it is surely the calm of one emerging from an experience that has been growing steadily more manic and disorientating. The crisis of identity is over. Each pair of the quartet fall into each other's arms with the usual symmetry, and Lady Bracknell and Jack share the curtain lines:

LADY BRACKNELL: My nephew, you seem to be displaying signs of triviality.

JACK: On the contrary, Aunt Augusta, I've now realised for the first time in my life the vital Importance of Being Earnest.

It is the recall to Lady Bracknell's world where 'trivial' and 'earnest' reverse the values the farce has been asserting. She has won, in a way: the nameless foundling whose very existence was subversive has been assimilated into the Establishment. His father a General, his aunt a Lady: the 'decencies of family life' are safe from the revolutionary horrors conjured up by the notion of being 'born, or at any rate, bred, in a hand-bag'. Yet we cannot be sure. The pun retains its teasing irony to the end. Jack speaks as an actor, looking out to the audience, slyly (never openly) sharing with them the joke closed from Lady Bracknell, that if there is a moral it is only the title for a farce. And the title reminds us that the farce is about being an actor, playing a part, being Earnest by 'realising' him, as actors and playwrights realise for their audiences the creations of their fantasy and everybody, in the long run, has to realise his own identity.

With *The Importance of Being Earnest* Wilde anticipated a major development in the twentieth century, the use of farce to make fundamentally serious (not earnest!) explorations into the realm of the irrational. The play has been immensely influential, serving as model for writers as diverse as T. S. Eliot, who gave a religious turn to the foundling motif in *The Confidential Clerk* (1953), and Charles Wood, in his bleakly funny play about the Second World War, *Dingo* (1969), which has British soldiers performing *The Importance of Being Earnest* in a German prison camp. Wilde's devotees, Joe Orton and Tom Stoppard, have paid especially full tribute to his genius. Orton, whose life had features in common with Wilde's, (homosexuality, traumatic experience of prison), said that his aim was to write a play as good as *The Importance of Being Earnest*. He came very near to doing this in *What the Butler Saw* (1969), a more manic version, in the vulgar postcard, sexy style proclaimed by its title, of Wilde's farce of identity: characters split into two, commandeer each other's identities, discover that they really are what they thought they were only pretending to be, in a way which continually acknowledges the Wildean source. While by 'borrowing' characters and whole episodes from *The Importance of Being Earnest* for his *Travesties*, Tom Stoppard demonstrates his belief that the play has entered the collective unconscious in the same way as the other masterpiece he uses in his own drama, *Hamlet*. Only if the play does indeed have that status, could the jokes of *Travesties* work to the full and the ruling ideas come over. *Travesties* is from first to last a piece of Wildean play on the relation between life and art in which everyone is juggling roles; Carr, who is never really in the play he thinks he is in, the Dadaist proclaiming 'Pleasure, pleasure', the girls who enact the tea-party scene line for line as if they did not know they were playing it, the ideal butler who turns out to be a secret Leninist and James Joyce playing an Irish comedian version of the real James Joyce who played in *The Importance of Being Earnest* in Zurich in 1917.

Wilde would surely have been amused by all this tongue-in-the-cheek play with his play. Still less can one doubt that he would have approved W. H. Auden's comment that *The Importance of Being Earnest* was 'the only pure verbal opera in English'.[11] In none of his plays, not even *Salomé*, is the musical treatment more pronounced. Verbal music is heightened by a host of musical devices and allusions; as in opera the curtain rises to the sound of music (Algernon's piano playing); Lady Bracknell contributes a Wagnerian peal and pays idiosyncratic tribute to the power of music by banning French songs from Algernon's concert programme; the spoken word moves irresistibly nearer the condition of music till the lovers are keeping the beat dictated by Gwendolen's uplifted forefinger, practically singing and dancing. Perhaps it is not surprising that actors have had difficulty in capturing this intricate stylisation. Modern actors may not make the same mistake as their Victorian predecessors – at least they know to keep a straight face – and no doubt many modern productions have come nearer to Wilde's conception than the first ones did. But they may also have become more stereotyped. Some famous performances have come to be thought of as definitive: Edith Evans' magnificently sonorous 'A hand-bag', Margaret Rutherford's piquantly obsessed Miss Prism, have established themselves rightly as high peaks in comic acting. These admired styles seem also to have fixed the pattern from which actors find it hard to move away. As Irving Wardle said of the 1982 National Theatre production, everyone was waiting to see how Judi Dench would handle the classic handbag line. Her low-key treatment (she concentrated on tearing up her notes on Jack's eligibility as a suitor) was in tune with a new conception of the role which preserved the veneer but allowed more of the human being to peep out from behind it.

Oscar Wilde

In the post-Orton world we might hope for performances of *The Importance of Being Earnest* that would take yet another line and realise the 'heartlessness' so troublesome to Shaw in bold, modern terms, bringing out the subversive and surreal elements. Such a production would have to end on a different note however, from the anarchic stupefaction of *What the Butler Saw*. Wilde does indeed, like Orton, show the world as tending to cruelty and heartlessness, life as an absurd performance, personality as a fluid thing, endlessly forming and reforming itself with the aid of masks (an emphasis on impermanence that alarmed even Yeats, the master of masks). But Wilde's optimistic, benevolent nature required a more harmonious ending for his farce than anything Orton, or perhaps any modern existentialist, would be likely to envisage. *The Importance of Being Earnest* ends with all the dissonances resolved and harmony achieved. It can only happen in Utopia, which means 'nowhere' – but as Wilde said, 'A map of the world that does not include Utopia is not worth even glancing at, for it leaves out the one country at which Humanity is always landing.'

9
Conclusion

On this high peak of achievement Wilde's career as a playwright closed. The ordeal that followed damaged his creative energy irretrievably. He made sporadic efforts to start new plays or work on those already started but the two long years of silence in prison had as he said kept his soul in bonds and he was never able to break through.

The fragments that survive must be mentioned: they have interest as suggestions of new developments, though it is difficult to estimate how far they might have succeeded. Among the pieces begun before the trial, *La Sainte Courtisane* had always given him trouble. In this ironical tale of a hermit and a courtesan who convert each other and in effect change places, Wilde could hear only one of the voices in the dialogue, so he told Charles Ricketts in 1895.[1] The courtesan said 'wonderful things' but the hermit was taciturn: 'I think I shall have to indicate his replies by stars or asterisks.' The curiously named play has obvious links with *Salomé*; the French title, the biblical rhythms, the duel between an ascetic and a sexually provocative woman, the symbolic emphasis on jewels (the sub-title of the fragment is 'The Woman Covered with Jewels'). Some critics have thought it was written with Sarah Bernhardt in mind, though that seems doubtful. What it does show is that Wilde was looking for a new way of expressing the idea demonstrated tragically in *Salomé*: an extreme of passion is drawn to its own opposite and the two can never be harmonised, only clash or reverse themselves. In *La Sainte Courtisane* he was aiming, it seems, at a witty treatment, along a line sketched to Beerbohm Tree: 'When you convert someone else to your own faith you cease to believe in it yourself.'

A similarly sardonic treatment of potentially tragic material was aimed at in another unfinished piece of the same period, *A Florentine Tragedy*. The manuscript of this play has a mysterious history (Hesketh Pearson thought a version had been completed and was among manuscripts stolen from Wilde's Tite Street home at the time of his arrest). In 1895 Wilde was proposing to send Alexander the 'vital parts' of his Florentine play; while in prison he tried in vain to work on it from memory and after his release, though frequently expressing his intention of finishing it, he never did so. This fragment too is based on ironical reversal, though of a darker, more emotional kind.[2] Wilde began with the ending and never got to the beginning: it was clearly the irony of the ending that intrigued him; the bourgeois husband discovering his wife being courted by the young aristocrat, drawing his sword on the lover, killing him and turning to attack his wife, to find her advancing with outstretched arms, 'dazed with wonder' at the transformation in her dull spouse:

BIANCA: Why
Did you not tell me you were so strong?

Conclusion

SIMONE: Why
    Did you not tell me you were beautiful?

The neatness of this suggests that Wilde saw the situation in a rather modern way as a black joke.

A witty, ironic treatment of sombre material was evidently a line that he would have pursued. Ross tells that in prison he invented two plays on biblical themes, 'Ahab and Isabel' and 'Pharaoh' which were 'similar' to *La Sainte Courtisane*: Ross thought 'Pharaoh' most original. It never materialised, nor did the two plays for which scenarios exist, 'The Cardinal of Avignon'[3] and an unnamed play of modern life, later written up by Frank Harris (to whom, along with several other unsuspecting patrons, Wilde sold the idea) as *Mr and Mrs Daventry*.

This modern scenario (*L*,360–2) shows Wilde making a very deliberate onslaught on the conventions of the *boulevard* theatre. It was to be a study in marital disharmony, ending in the triumphant self-emancipation of the wife. *A Doll's House* type of triumph, but more complete, for Wilde's heroine acquires a lover as well as her freedom. In the fourth act wife and lover discuss *Frou-Frou*, a celebrated *boulevard* play with a nauseating morality, about a woman who leaves her husband for a lover and is punished by being banned from seeing her child until she is in the last stage of a mortal illness, when she returns to the marital home to make a suitably repentant death. Wilde's heroine ignores the warning, proclaims not just her need of love but her right to it – and has her claim endorsed by her playwright.

The pains he took over such fine detail reveal a Wilde very different from the careless wit of legend, tossing off epigrams regardless of dramatic appropriateness. In looking back over his career as playwright, and considering how his plays have fared since with performers, audiences and critics, I think it is clear that people have often been misled by the lightness of his touch, the art with which he conceals his art. As one of his most serious admirers, John Luis Borges, says, 'his work is so harmonious that it may seem inevitable and even trite'.[4]

Performers have always had difficulty in finding the right style. Either they have over-stressed the caricature, as Fanny Brough did in the first production of *A Woman of No Importance*. Shaw said she made 'an eminently possible person quite impossible'. Or they have played too realistically, in which vein Canon Chasuble as a minutely realistic character study of a country clergyman must be the *ne plus ultra*. It is obviously not easy to strike the right balance between the realistic psychology and the fantastic stylisation, the aristocratic grandeur and the mischievous wit. One of the most accomplished of all John Worthings, John Gielgud, has told how he discovered very late in his career that he had always taken the muffin scene too fast. 'I believe I've been wrong about this scene whenever I have played it,' he told Robert Flemyng when they were doing it for a benefit performance. They slowed it down and drew far more laughs by eating the muffins 'with real solemnity'. Only at the stage where he thought he had finished with the play for ever did this consummate actor realise that the muffin scene easily degenerated into knockabout and must be acted very slowly, for the play 'is like chamber music. You must not indulge yourself or caricature.'[5] This brings home the difficulty – which lesser actors (and directors) often fail even to identify. Film and television add new problems, the former with its wish for sumptuousness (amply displayed in the film of *An Ideal Husband*), television with its preference for realism. Yet the right style can be found, so Gielgud himself has demonstrated – and Edith Evans and the many other actors from Rose Leclerq as the first Lady Bracknell – who were prepared to take Wilde's art as seriously as their own.

On the scenic side, there is a similar challenge which has been even less recognised. Few, it may be assumed, have seen Wilde's subtle stage designs fully realised, had their attention drawn to the delicate symbolism of the terrace in *Lady Windermere's Fan* and *A Woman of No Importance* or the Boucher tapestry in *An Ideal Husband*. Even Rex Whistler, whose décor for the Chilterns' octagon room had the right kind of airy grandeur, substituted a vast portrait (presumably of Lady Windermere) for the 'Triumph of Love' which was meant to be a visual key to the play's meaning. Sumptuousness has often replaced Wilde's austere scenic plans. He certainly advised would-be producers that his plays required expensive accessories, beautiful clothes and so forth; the visual effect had to be perfect. But he did not mean by that ornateness such as Cecil Beaton proposed for a production of *Lady Windermere's Fan* in 1945, when the scene was to be 'overcharged, richly stuffed and embroidered with a great use of *trompe l'oeil* and *enfilades* in false perspectives of Victorian stucco and heavy chandeliers.'[6] No wonder John Gielgud, directing, seemed 'a bit overwhelmed'. The feeling for style in this production was so uncertain that there were actually plans to transfer the delicately intimate scene between Lady Windermere and Lord Darlington in the first act from the morning room to the incongruously grand ballroom setting of the second act: fortunately they realised in time that Wilde knew better and went back to his directions.

In the opera house, that meeting place of all the arts, *Salomé* has had rather better fortune. Costumes by Salvador Dali in Peter Brook's production of the Strauss work may not have been to all tastes; but the commissioning of a major artist for the task showed that the importance of the visual element in the total effect was fully recognised. It would be hard, of course, to present *Salomé* without some sense of its scenic symbolism; in the plays of modern life, it seems, visual hints are more easily overlooked.

In conclusion it may be said that Wilde's plays are crying out for bold, imaginative recreation, for their modern 'after-life', in Jonathan Miller's phrase. It is time to forget the nineteenth century idea of them which has lingered on into our era: in any case, it fell far short of Wilde's more modern thought. There are many things we should be able to hope for, nowadays: a *Salomé* (minus Strauss) which aims at the synthesis of arts dreamed of by Wilde; an *Importance of Being Earnest* which catches the existential note; a well-orchestrated *Lady Windermere's Fan*, and almost any intelligent production of *A Woman of No Importance*, that most strangely neglected of the major plays. Possibly the melodrama which is so much part of the last-named work frightens potential directors. That is a symptom of the uncertainty and uneasiness about style which has so often inhibited not only performances but criticism of Wilde. Yet it is the only way in which his plays can be interpreted – to grasp the style. 'Everything matters in art except the subject' is no idle jest but the key Wilde offers to a true understanding of his dramatic art.

References

1. A Modern Perspective on Wilde as Man of Theatre

1. G. B. Shaw, *Dramatic Opinions and Essays*, vol. 1, London, 1913, pp. 11–15.
2. For this and other quotations cited from the same source, see 'The Soul of Man under Socialism', *Works*, pp. 1018–43.
3. Letter of 1 April 1897 from Reading Prison, to Robert Ross, *Letters*, p. 512.
4. 'The Decay of Lying', *Works*, pp. 909–31. First published in 1889 (*Nineteenth Century*); a revised version appeared in *Intentions*, 1891.
5. For this and other quotations cited from the same source, see 'De Profundis', *Letters*, pp. 423–511.
6. *Pall Mall Gazette*, 22 February 1892.
7. I. Fletcher, *Romantic Mythologies*, p. 195.
8. See J. Stokes, 'A Wagner Theatre: Professor Herkomer's Pictorial-Musical Plays' in *Resistible Theatres*, pp. 69–110.
9. *Dramatic Review*, 22 May 1886.
10. *Oscar Wilde: Recollections by Jean Paul Raymond and Charles Ricketts* (written by Ricketts, using J. P. Raymond as pseudonym), p. 40.
11. Interview for *St James's Gazette*, 18 January 1895. Mikhail, p. 249.
12. This, and quotation from James p. 17 in H. James, *The Scenic Art*, ed. A. Wade, pp. 261–81.
13. Clement Scott, *Illustrated London News*, 27 February 1892. Beckson, p. 126.

14. W. Archer, *The Theatrical World for 1893*, 1894.

15. G. B. Shaw, preface to *The Philanderer*, Plays Unpleasant, (Penguin), p. 14.

2. 'Vera or The Nihilists'

1. *The World* (London), 30 November 1881.

2. See R. Hingley, *The Nihilists*, to which I am indebted for information on these aspects of the movement.

3. *New York Tribune*, 21 August 1883. Beckson, pp. 55–8.

4. G. A. Sala, *Echoes of the Year Eighteen Hundred and Eighty-Three*, 1884.

5. G. B. Shaw, *Dramatic Opinions and Essays*, p. 117.

6. *The World* (New York) 12 August 1883. Mikhail, pp. 114–16.

3. 'The Duchess of Padua'

1. This and other passages quoted from the letter to Mary Anderson (23 March 1883) are in *Letters*, pp. 135–42.

2. 'Shakespeare and Stage Costume', published in 1885 (*Nineteenth Century*), was republished, slightly revised, as 'The Truth of Masks' in *Intentions*, 1891.

4. 'Salomé'

1. *Pall Mall Budget* (London), XL, 30 June 1892. Mikhail, pp. 186–8.

2. *Pall Mall Gazette*, 1 July 1892.

3. Lugné-Poe directed the play at the Théâtre de l'Oeuvre with himself as Herod and Lina Munte as Salomé. It was favourably reviewed, for instance by Henri Bauer in the *Echo de Paris*.

4. *The Times*, 23 Feburary 1893.

5. P. Jullian, *Oscar Wilde*, p. 209.

6. *St James's Gazette*, 18 January 1895. Mikhail, p. 249.

7. *Pall Mall Budget*. Mikhail, p. 188.

8. *Pall Mall Budget*. Mikhail, p. 188.

9. C. S. Nassaar, *Into the Demon Universe*, p. 84.

10. See S. Weintraub, *Beardsley*, p. 73.

11. Robert Ross, introduction to *Salomé and A Florentine Tragedy*, p. xi.

12. W. Graham Robertson, *Time Was*, pp. 125–7.

13. *Oscar Wilde: Recollections by Jean Paul Raymond and Charles Ricketts* (written by Ricketts, using J. P. Raymond as pseudonym), p. 53.

14. P. Jullian, *Oscar Wilde*, p. 215.

15. Gomez Carrillo, 'Comment Oscar Wilde rêva Salome', *La Plume* (Paris) 1902. Mikhail, pp. 192–5.

16. M. Beerbohm, *Around Theatres*, p. 379.

5. 'Lady Windermere's Fan'

1. Report by 'First-Nighter', *Pall Mall Gazette*, 22 February 1892.

2. Among the many sources suggested for *Lady Windermere's Fan* were: Dumas fils, *L'Etrangère* and *Françillon*: Scribe, *Adrienne Lecouvreur*; Haddon Chambers, *The Idler* (which features a fan). The unnamed reviewer in *Black and White* (27 February 1892) thought Wilde's play a cross between the last named, *Françillon*, and the *Eden* of Edgar Saltus.

3. Wilde's argument with Alexander over his wish to keep Mrs Erlynne's secret till the end of the play had support from some reviewers, for instance A. B. Walkley who shared Wilde's pleasure in the suspense created by withholding the vital information. Wilde professed to be converted in the end by friends who thought the psychological interest would be increased by placing the revelation earlier. *Letters*, pp. 308–9.

4. R. Shewan, *Oscar Wilde: Art and Egotism*, p. 67.

6. 'A Woman of No Importance'

1. G. Burgess, '*An Ideal Husband* at the Haymarket Theatre: A Talk with Oscar Wilde' in *The Sketch*, 9 January 1895. Mikhail, p. 241.

2. *Illustrated London News*, 29 April 1893.

3. C. E. Montague, *Dramatic Values*, p. 178.

4. M. Beerbohm, *More Theatres*, p. 334.

5. Janet Achurch (the first English Nora) played Hester Prynne in her husband's adaptation of Hawthorne's *The Scarlet Letter* at the Olympic Theatre in June 1888.

6. *The Saturday Review*, 6 May 1893. Beckson, p. 154.

7. W. Archer, *The World*, 26 April 1893; repeated in *The Theatrical World for 1893*, Beckson, p. 146.

7. 'An Ideal Husband'

1. W. Archer, *Pall Mall Budget*, 10 January 1895, repeated in *The Theatrical World of 1895*. Beckson, p. 174.

2. Clement Scott noted the similarities between the plots of *An Ideal*

Husband and Victorien Sardou's *Dora, Illustrated London News*, 12 January 1895. Beckson, pp. 178–9.

3. G. Burgess, *The Sketch*, 9 January 1895. Mikhail, p. 241.

4. All quotations from Shaw in *Dramatic Opinions and Essays*, pp. 11–15.

5. See *Letters*, p. 339 footnote 2 for the gloss on this numbering supplied by Hesketh Pearson.

6. A. B. Walkley, *The Speaker*, 12 January 1895. Beckson, p. 179.

8. 'The Importance of Being Earnest'

1. M. McCarthy, 'The Unimportance of Being Oscar' in R. Ellmann, ed. *Oscar Wilde: A Collection of Critical Essays*, pp. 107–10.

2. For this and other quotations from the same source, see, 'The Soul of Man under Socialism', *Works*, pp. 1018–43.

3. *St James's Gazette*, 18 January 1895. Mikhail, p. 250.

4. G. B. Shaw, *Dramatic Opinions and Essays*, pp. 32–5.

5. M. Beerbohm, *Around Theatres*, pp. 188–91.

6. The fullest edition of the four-act version is S. A. Dickson, ed. 2 vols, New York Public Library, Arents Tobacco Collection Publication no. 6, 1956. An English edition was edited by V. Holland, 1957. The Gribsby episode is printed in the New Mermaids edition of the play.

7. See D. Parker, 'Oscar Wilde's Great Farce: *The Importance of Being Earnest*', *Modern Language Quarterly*, vol. 35, No 2, June 1974.

8. P. K. Cohen, *The Moral Vision of Oscar Wilde*, pp. 201–3.

9. C. E. Montague, *Dramatic Values*, p. 186.

10. See R. Jackson, ed., *The Importance of Being Earnest*, for references to the drafts.

11. W. H. Auden, 'An Improbable Life: Review of *Letters of Oscar Wilde*', *New Yorker*, 9 March 1963. Ellman, pp. 116–37.

9. Conclusion

1. *Recollections of Oscar Wilde by Jean Paul Raymond*, (Charles Ricketts), p. 40.

2. See A. Bird, *The Plays of Oscar Wilde*, p. 199.

3. The Scenario of 'The Cardinal of Avignon' is included in 'Stuart Mason' (Christopher Millard), *Bibliography of Oscar Wilde*, pp. 583–5.

4. J. L. Borges, 'About Oscar Wilde', *Other Inquisitions 1937–1952*, 1964. Ellmann, pp. 172–4.

5. J. Gielgud, *An Actor and his Time*, p. 158.

6. Cecil Beaton, *Self Portrait, With Friends: The Selected Diaries of Cecil Beaton, 1927–1974*, p. 167.

Bibliography

Notes on Editions

Except where otherwise indicated, the following editions of Wilde's work have been used for quotation and reference:

The Works of Oscar Wilde, ed. G. F. Maine (Collins, 1948). Referred to as *Works*.

Salomé and a Florentine Tragedy, with introduction by Robert Ross (Methuen, 1908) (for the French text of *Salomé*).

The Importance of Being Earnest, ed. R. Jackson, New Mermaids edn, (Benn, 1980).

Lady Windermere's Fan, ed. I. Small, New Mermaids edn (Benn, 1980).

The Original Four-Act Version of The Importance of Being Earnest (Methuen, 1957).

The Letters of Oscar Wilde, ed. R. Hart-Davis (Hart-Davis, 1963). Referred to in text as *L*.

Place of publication is London, except where otherwise indicated.

Select Book List

Allan, M., *My Life and Dancing* (Everett, 1908).

Oscar Wilde

Archer, W., *The Theatrical World of 1893–7* (Walter Scott, 1894–8).

Beerbohm, M., *Around Theatres* (Hart-Davis, 1953).

——, *More Theatres* (Hart-Davis, 1969).

——, *Last Theatres* (Hart-Davis, 1970).

Beckson, K., *Oscar Wilde: The Critical Heritage* (Routledge and Kegan Paul, 1970).

Bird, A., *The Plays of Oscar Wilde* (Vision Press, 1977).

Cohen, P. K., *The Moral Vision of Oscar Wilde* (New Jersey and London: Associated University Presses, 1978).

Douglas, A., *Oscar Wilde: a Summing Up* (Duckworth, 1940).

Duncan, B., *The St James's Theatre* (Barrie and Rockliff, 1964).

Ellmann, R. ed., *The Artist as Critic: Critical Writings of Oscar Wilde* (W. H. Allen, 1970).

—— ed., *Oscar Wilde, a Collection of Critical Essays* (New Jersey: Prentice-Hall, 1969).

'Michael Field', *Works and Days: From the Journal of Michael Field*, ed. T. and D. C. Sturge Moore (John Murray, 1933).

Findlater, R., *Banned!* (MacGibbon and Kee, 1967).

Fletcher, I., *Romantic Mythologies* (1967).

—— ed., *Decadence and the 1890s*, Stratford-upon-Avon Studies 17 (Edward Arnold, 1979).

Gielgud, J., *An Actor and his Time* (Sidgwick and Jackson, 1979).

Hingley, R., *The Nihilists* (Weidenfeld and Nicholson, 1967).

Holland, V., *Oscar Wilde and his World* (Thames and Hudson, 1978).

James, H., *The Scenic Art*, ed. A. Wade (Hart-Davis, 1949).

Jullian, P., *Oscar Wilde* (Granada Publishing, 1971).

——, *Dreamers of Decadence*, (Phaidon Press, 1971). Originally published as *Esthètes et Magiciens* (Paris, 1969).

Kermode, F., *Romantic Image* (Routledge and Kegan Paul, 1957).

——, *Modern Essays* (Fontana, 1971).

Marshall, N., *The Other Theatre* (John Lehmann, 1947).

——, *The Masque Library* (Curtain Press, 1950).

Mason, A. E., *Sir George Alexander and the St James's Theatre*, (Macmillan, 1935; reprinted New York and London: Benjamin Blom, 1969).

'Stuart Mason' (C. S. Millard), *Bibliography of Oscar Wilde* (1908; reprinted Bertram Rota, 1967).

Mikhail, E. H., *Oscar Wilde: Interviews and Recollections*, 2 vols (Macmillan, 1979).

Montague, C. E., *Dramatic Values* (Chatto and Windus, 1941).

Nassaar, C. S., *Into the Demon Universe* (New Haven and London: Yale University Press, 1974).

Pearson, H., *The Life of Oscar Wilde* (Methuen, 1946; reprinted 1954).

Peters, M., *Bernard Shaw and the Actresses* (New York: Doubleday, 1980).

Bibliography

Pope, W. Macqueen, *Haymarket: Theatre of Perfection* (W. H. Allen, 1948).

——, *St James's: Theatre of Distinction* (W. H. Allen, 1958).

Ricketts, C., *Pages on Art* (Constable, 1913).

——, *Oscar Wilde: Recollections by Jean Paul Raymond and Charles Ricketts* (1932) (written by Ricketts, using J. P. Raymond as pseudonym).

Robertson, W. Graham, *Time Was* (Hamish Hamilton, 1931; reprinted Quartet Books, 1981).

Shaw, G. B., *Dramatic Opinions and Essays*, 2 vols (Constable, 1913).

Shewan, R., *Oscar Wilde: Art and Egotism* (Macmillan, 1977).

Stokes, J., *Oscar Wilde* (Writers and their Work No. 264) (1978).

——, *Resistible Theatres* (Paul Elek Books, 1972).

Symons, A., *A Study of Oscar Wilde* (Charles Sawyer, 1930).

Taranow, G., *Sarah Bernhardt* (New Jersey: Princeton U.P., 1972).

Weintraub, S., *Beardsley* (Penguin, rev. 1972).

Worth, K., *The Irish Drama of Europe from Yeats to Beckett* (Athlone Press, 1978).

Index

Index

Index

Index